PURPOSE DRIVEN

#! Stay Purpose Driven !!

PUBLICATIONS

LOURAWLS NAIRN, JR.

Cover Design: ETA & Associates

Page Design & Layout Design: OA. Blueprints, LLC

Edited by: ETA & Associates

Printed in the United States of America

ISBN: 978-1-942499-10-7

CONTENTS

ACKNOWLEDGMENTS

Growing up, I never saw myself writing a book. It was never even a thought of mine. I realize now that the things we never imagine ourselves doing are the ones that could have the most impact on other people's lives. There were times when I questioned myself, "Should I write this book?" Then I came to the conclusion that if I did not write it, I could be doing a disservice to many people whose lives could be positively impacted by it. I want to acknowledge everyone who helped me and supported me throughout this process.

I wish to thank my parents, Monalisa McKinney and Lourawls Nairn, Sr., for all their constant love and support. To my younger brother, Laquan Nairn, for always having my back and believing in me. I love you all dearly.

To Cierra Seay, my gifted creative writing coach: Thank you for helping me with this project and I look forward to working with you again very soon. I also wish to thank my mentor, Dr. Eric Thomas: Thank you for always being there for me and encouraging me to write this book more than anyone.

To all my family, friends, coaches, teammates and loved ones: Thank you all for your love and support throughout my journey.

May God bless and keep you all, and may you all be Purpose Driven!

INTRODUCTION

Many times in life we go through certain situations that don't make any sense to us. We try to figure everything out on our own instead of going to our Heavenly Father—our greatest source. My life was full of challenges and problems that made me who I am today. The only power they had was the power I gave them. Although sometimes those tribulations held me hostage, I never let them defeat me. Going through these situations helped me figure out who I was and what God placed me on this earth to do. Everything He put me through was preparing me for what He was about to bring me to. Did I question Him? Yes. Did I fail? Absolutely, I stumbled so many times. Did I give up? No way! The Bible tells us in Romans 5:3-4: *Not only so, but we also glory in our sufferings, because we know that suffering produces perseverance; perseverance, character; and character, hope.* These sufferings are trials and trials are never meant to break us but to make us.

With the power of God, I was able to get through and will continue to get through all that life throws at me. He was my strength in every situation I ever faced. Everything I ever had to endure, because of Him, I came out victorious. It is not about what I did, it is about what He did through me for His glory. There was not a day that He wasn't with me. There wasn't a trial I faced that was bigger than Him. There wasn't a time I prayed that He didn't hear me. He showed His power through me. He made other kids in my neighborhood believe that they could do whatever they wanted to do and become whoever they wanted to be because of what He was doing in my life. I'll bet He is doing the same in your life. I couldn't understand why I was going through what I was going through. Frustration would be at an all-time high. I would ask God, "Why would you put me through this or that?" "Why me, God?" He would say, "Why not you?" Most of the time we are afraid of what we do not understand. I now realize that everything I went through was not for me but for those who I was born to reach.

I wrote this book to give you the tools and principles that I used to get through the toughest times of my life. I would not be where I am today without them. These principles took me from playing basketball on broken glass and rocks in The Bahamas to playing in front of over 70,000 people in the Final Four. I pray that you all be encouraged by this book and that it helps you to understand that it doesn't matter who brought you into this world, where you were born, who you are or what you did, God can and will still use you.

CHAPTER 1

Purpose Baby

A woman being pregnant is one of the most beautiful things in life. It changes everything about the woman over those nine months and sometimes shorter than that. During the pregnancy stage, women talk about the baby all the time—wondering whether it will be a boy or girl, shopping for baby clothes, thinking of names, talking to the baby, etc. They have this inexplicable joy about a person they have never met before. It is normal to love someone that you've consistently been around, but where it gets interesting is when you love someone you have never met before. It is a love that is unexplainable. Although she is carrying the child, she does not know who she's carrying. Most importantly, she does not own who she's carrying. The Bible tells us that God knitted us together in our mother's womb. So, in all actuality, the baby is His. He placed the baby in the mother's womb and He already knows what the child will become. However, the mother doesn't know. I can bet you all the money in the world that Gloria James, the mother of LeBron James, did not know she was carrying one of the greatest players to ever play the game of basketball. Alberta Williams King, the mother of Martin Luther King, Jr., did not know she was carrying a dream—a dream that we all live today. What about Sir Isaac Newton's mother, Hannah Ayscough? She had no idea she was carrying the laws of gravity. All the people I mentioned had an impact on history that cannot be ignored. LeBron James is still impacting history today. Just like all their mothers, I wonder who your mother was carrying. There is something so special on the inside of you and if you are willing to pay the price of bringing it out, history won't be able to ignore it. However, what you're experiencing right now may be telling you otherwise. Don't let what you're going through make you believe you're not special.

There was this 16-year-old from Nassau, Bahamas who was living with her mother when she became pregnant. She had planned to attend college but that dream was over when she found out she was expecting. Her mother had her at the age of 17, so she knew she wouldn't be happy to hear about her pregnancy. She was too afraid to tell her mom, so she decided to tell her grandmother. One of her mother's greatest fears was that her daughter would make the same mistake she did. When her mother found out, she was so furious that she forgot she also had gotten pregnant at the same age. Her emotions blinded her to the fact that she did the same thing. Finally calming down, she realized that she was mad about the very thing she did. However, no parent wants their children to make the same mistakes they did because they want better for them. Also, when the same mistakes have been made, parents tend to let their emotions get in the way and they forget that they were once in the same boat. Parents expect you to be different from them, although you have never seen different. So, what it takes is extreme discipline and determination to not make the same mistakes your parents made. However, what will help is if your parents open up about their past. You can never know the things you should try to avoid in your life, if you don't know the things they couldn't avoid in theirs. Most parents expect their children to do the opposite of what they did without having any knowledge of what that was.

Before getting pregnant, this teenager's doctors told her she would never be able to have kids because of her sickle cell anemia. They told her that it would be too risky for her to have kids. I just think about how all women grow up talking about how bad they want to have kids one day; To walk into a doctor's office and hear that you might never be able to have kids can be devastating to a young woman. Even though she knew that having a baby could literally kill her, she still had no idea just what would happen to her during pregnancy.

The first three months of her pregnancy, she would wake up every morning around 5 am to throw up. The only thing she could eat without throwing up was McDonald's and ice. She could keep nothing else down. Heading into her fourth month of pregnancy, she started going to a specialty clinic because she was what they called a "high-risk pregnancy" due to her sickle cell disease. I imagine this being very scary for a mother who was told she would never be able to have kids. I'm sure thoughts about the doctor being right and thoughts about her possibly dying crept in frequently but the thought of losing her baby was something she could not handle. Doubt kicked in many times walking into a specialty clinic thinking about how they said she wouldn't be able to have kids. However, she was going to a specialty clinic because who she was carrying was very rare; so rare that the baby needed special attention. The doctors were not the only ones giving the baby special attention. In the book of Psalms, chapter 139:13-16, the verses talk about how God knitted us in our mother's womb, how our frames were not hidden from Him, and how His eyes saw our unformed bodies, which means that God is always watching a pregnant woman.

During her fifth month of pregnancy, the vomiting slowly went away. However, vomiting was replaced by constant pain that was unbearable. This was too much for the teenager to handle. Although she was experiencing pain, she also realized how happy the baby was. He was full of energy and life and would use the walls of her stomach as a punching bag to kick her continuously. As soon as she thought everything was about to slow down, by the seventh month of her pregnancy, she became bedridden. Isn't life that way? As soon as things seem like they are starting to get better, here comes another hurdle. She would bleed constantly for the last two months of her pregnancy. The doctors watched her very closely and they became very concerned. The concern was that the baby she was carrying might not make it out alive. Another concern was that giving birth to this baby could kill her. The teenager and the baby's father had gotten married after finding out she was pregnant. In the early morning hours of October 8, 1994, she woke up with a nosebleed and an excruciating headache. She woke her husband, her mother and her aunt to get dressed and take her to the Princess Margaret Hospital in The Bahamas. When she arrived at the hospital, they immediately took her to a room to take her blood pressure. Her blood pressure was extremely high and all she could do was cry. Lying down in the bed and reciting the Lord's Prayer, she could hear the nurse talking about how high her blood pressure was. As the nurse was explaining, she began to feel nauseous and asked for a bucket so she could vomit. She then went into labor. During labor, as she pushed and pushed she started having a seizure. She then passed out and the doctors had to cut her open in order to bring the baby into the world. Sometimes in order to bring out what is inside of you, you have to be cut. Eventually the wound from being cut will turn into a scar, which is a healed wound and a permanent reminder of what you had to go through to get where you are. But that takes some time. Giving birth to this baby was so hard on her body that it completely shut down. She was pregnant with purpose and the purpose of this baby was so powerful that it almost killed her.

She then spent two weeks in a coma, which was one of the scariest things she'd ever gone through. When she got out of the coma, she thought a lot about what the doctor had said to her about not being able to have kids because of her sickness. Complications continued. Her blood pressure was still extremely high; she had swelling in her limbs and a feeling of movement inside of her that she thought was another baby. These com-plications caused the doctors to run another series of tests on her. They also did an ultrasound and found out that, while in the coma, the afterbirth had been left inside of her. The doctors then had to go back inside of her to clean it out. This caused her to stay in the hos-pital for another three months. As crazy and abnormal as this was, God was in control the whole time. His plans were much greater than the report of the doctor. Nothing against the doctor, he was just doing his job.

But when God has a plan, as Proverbs 19:21 says, "His purpose will prevail." The teenager lost so much weight because of everything she went through while carrying and giving birth to this baby. She only weighed about ninety pounds. She was not the same after giving birth to the baby. That is what happens when you bring out what is inside of you. You will not be the same. Everything will change. You look different. You walk different. You talk different. You act different. Above all, you begin to appreciate life more because what was on the inside of you was so powerful, that bringing it out of you almost killed you. But there is a saying that goes, "What doesn't kill you, makes you stronger."

At this point, the teenager had never seen or touched the baby, which for a mom may be the worst experience ever. After a woman gives birth, the first person the doctor gives the baby to is the mother. However, in this situation, that was not the case. Because she had the seizure during childbirth and then went into a coma, she did not see the baby until the baby was four months old. The baby boy went home with his father. The father took extremely good care of his newborn son. He was so protective of his baby boy that he would give the baby baths in drinking water and also wash his clothes in drinking water. Who was this baby who almost killed his mother? Who had to be watched closely because of his mother's illness and who could possibly not make it into the world as a result? Whose father bathed him in drinking water? Why did his mother have to go through all of that just to bring him into the world? It was because his mother wasn't just pregnant with a baby, she was pregnant with purpose.

Each and every one of us is pregnant with purpose. In order for us to bring forth that purpose, we have to go through pain and experience things we never imagined. Sometimes bringing forth that purpose can almost kill us because of the power of it. However, it won't. We will never give birth to our purpose hanging around listening to those who want us to abort it—meaning that there are some people who will try and stop you from becoming who you were born to be. Don't allow them to make you kill what is on the inside of you. People who aborted their purpose will want you to abort yours. There are people with PhD's in making others abort their purposes. In other words, some people have mastered making others kill what is inside of them. Put yourself around people who, for the sake of their purpose, endure the pain of giving birth. Also place yourself around those who will give life to your purpose. Birthing your purpose is going to hurt. You are going to want to give up. You are going to feel like you can't make it. But all of that pain is connected to giving life to what you're called to be and do. By the way, that young girl who got pregnant when she was 16 years old and almost died giving birth to the baby is my mother, Monalisa McKinney. The young man who bathed and washed the baby's clothes in drinking water is my father, Lourawls Nairn, Sr. The baby is me.

Purpose Principles

1. Sometimes in order to bring out what is inside of you, you have to be cut.

2. There is something so special on the inside of you that if you are willing to pay the price of bringing it out, history won't be able to ignore it.

3. Don't let your emotions make you forget similar mistakes you've made.

4. Don't allow people to make you kill your purpose because they killed theirs.

5. Put yourself around people who, for the sake of their purpose, endure the pain of giving birth.

CHAPTER 2

I Don't Live There

The environment you grow up in doesn't make you, you make the environment. Also, it doesn't matter where you live or how you live, someone else always has it worse than you do. In essence, no matter what your environment is, be grateful that you have it and use it to help make you who you want to be.

As we were growing up, my little brother, Laquan, and I were very close. He followed me everywhere I went. Also, it did not matter what I was doing, good or bad, he would do it simply because I was doing it. My parents dressed us alike from head to toe; Most of the time, people who did not know us would think we were twins. My dad always made sure my brother and I had anything we wanted and all the things we needed. We had the best shoes, the best clothes, all of our school supplies and the best school uniforms, which was a lot more than many of the kids at school had. All the kids at school naturally assumed we had everything. They would see our clothes, shoes and how we were always dressed alike and ask, "How big is your house?" I always switched the subject when that question came up because even though we had all of those nice things, the one thing we were embarrassed about was the house we lived in.

Anytime we were having conversations in school about things we had, what our parents did, where we live and so on, I never brought up our house. That was something I did the best I could to avoid talking about. I felt like if my friends or people at school knew where I lived and how the house looked, they would laugh at me. I imagined all the things they would say such as, "Maybe y'all should take the money you spend on shoes to get a better house," or "Would you rather have nice clothes or your own bed to sleep in?" These were questions I was very afraid of. I never told my parents about the feelings and fears I was having. I figured they would tell me not to worry about what other people say, but that wouldn't have stopped me from being embarrassed. The first house we lived in was a one-bedroom house with a small area with a toilet in it, no carpet, no running water, and we took baths outside in a round, tin tub. Even though it was hot in The Bahamas, taking a bath outside felt so cold. We also had to put buckets all around the house because whenever it would rain, the roof would leak.

My dad slept with his head at one end, I slept with my head at the other end, and my mother and brother did the same thing. We also had a really small kitchen area. There was a little table that my brother and I would sit at to eat our food, using crates or buckets as our chairs. Some nights a rat would crawl over us while we slept. It was hard living there. The house was incredibly tiny. We only had two doors in the entire house. There was a front door and a backdoor. I can remember the house like it was yesterday. One day, one of my friends asked me to show him where I lived and I took him to my godmother's house. I walked past the house I was actually living in and took him to a house that was not mine. Then when we were walking back and passed my house, I told him that my actual house was a place I had to myself. I told him that nobody else lived there with me. I felt so bad that I lied but the embarrassment and my pride took over. If my parents had ever found out I lied to my friend like that, it would have been bad for me. To this day, they still don't know about this. They won't find out until they read this book.

While living in this house, none of my friends ever came over. We never had sleepovers or friends just coming to hangout. Even if we wanted to, there was no way possible we could have friends over. The condition and size of the house made it impossible. Even though I was embarrassed about letting my friends know where I lived, I never complained about our living conditions.

Some of the scariest times living in that house was when we had tropical storms or when we would catch a little piece of a hurricane. Fear was present all the time with us wondering if our house was strong enough to take a hit from the hurricane and survive. This was where the leaking roof came in. We would put buckets all around the house to help with the leaking. The roof would leak anytime it rained but it was worse if there were tropical storms or hurricanes in the area.

How you live doesn't really matter when you are living with people you love deeply and who deeply love you. Even though the house wasn't so great, we had each other and we made it work. I wasn't ashamed of who I was, I was ashamed of where I lived. That is a huge difference. No matter where you live or how you live, you shouldn't be ashamed of who you are. This situation prepared me to live in any situation and be able to make the most of what I have. Sometimes we want more than we have or better than what we have when what we have may actually be the only things we need to be happy. Maybe we would not have been happy had we had a better housing situation. We might have found our happiness in the house instead of what really matters: having each other. This is where I began to find motivation. I would think to myself that I was going to do whatever it took to make sure my first house would be 100 times better than my first childhood house. I started to imagine myself having a family and seeing my kids running around the living room and chasing each other around the entire house. Even though I saw that in my heart, when I would look around, it seemed impossible that I could actually get what I imagined. I believed I could, but when I looked around I would say to myself, "Who do I have to look up to and say he did it or she did it, so I can?" I also said I would make sure my family and I would be tight no matter what. As long as we have each other, we can make it through anything. I knew my parents wanted to live in a better house, but I never heard them complain about it. They just took great care of my brother and me and did what they had to do. Every day, I think about that house I lived in. I also think about what it is going to be like when I own my first home. How I am going to just look around and think about what it used to feel like to be in a house so small. Many may say, "How were you so motivated at such a young age?" I say to those people, "Why do I have to be a certain age to be motivated?" Your age shouldn't determine how motivated you are. What you went through should determine how motivated you are. Don't put an age on when to start being motivated. Let what you experienced drive you to make sure you never experience what you went through again. Just because you lived a certain way growing up, doesn't mean you have to live that way as an adult. You get to choose whether you do or not. You may not get to choose what kind of house you grow up in, but you can make the choice, at any age, to have a better house someday. You won't be able to change it by wishing for it. The only way you will change it is by working for it.

While living in this small house, something else started to happen. My mom and my dad would always get into heated arguments. The house was so small that my brother and I could hear everything that was going on. There wasn't anywhere for my brother and me to go so we had to sit there and listen. The events that would happen after this would change our family.

Purpose Principles

1. Your environment doesn't make you, you make your environment.

2. Don't be embarrassed of what you have; someone always has it worse than you.

3. When pride takes over, it will make you lie.

4. In any environment, family can make it if they stick together.

5. Let what you go through motivate you.

CHAPTER 3

Turn the Negative into Positive

My grandmother, Rebecca McKinney, and my Aunt Cibby, may her soul rest in peace, always liked my dad. This all changed before I was born when my grandmother started hearing rumors about how my dad was treating my mom. She would hear rumors of my dad hitting my mom and that didn't sit well with her at all.

As a child I saw for myself what my grandmother had heard about. Arguments in our house were heated, late at night, sometimes throughout the day and there wasn't anywhere my brother and I could go to hide from it. I hated to hear my parents argue and see my dad hit my mom. This absolutely broke my heart. I would think to myself, "How could you do that to someone you love?" After every fight, my mom would always leave for a few weeks and then she and my father would end up back together. My brother and I would always stay with our dad because our mom couldn't take care of us on her own. This was hard for me, especially being the oldest child. I love both of my parents deeply, but seeing my mom go through the abuse, really rocked my world. It did the same exact thing to my brother. My job as an older brother was to make sure I was always there for my brother in every situation, but even more when things were bad between mom and dad. After they would fight, the next day, my brother and I would be walking to school talking about what happened and how much it hurt us to see our mom go through it. Not having my mom around the house sometimes was very weird for my brother and me because a house that once felt complete would feel incomplete. I also saw how not having my mom around sometimes would weigh on my dad.

My relationship with my mom is everything to me. For as long as I can remember, no one has ever meant to me what my mom has meant to me. We have a relationship that is very hard to explain. For me to see her go through all the fighting and then not live with us sometimes was very hard. Seeing her pack her stuff and then walk out the door; I often wondered sometimes if she would ever come back. The fighting continued and it became very difficult for me to deal with. It was so hard, that at times, it would be the only thing I thought about when I was in school. I would be at school physically, but mentally I was out of it because my mind was focused on what was going on at home.

I never told my parents how much it was affecting me, although I'm pretty sure they knew that neither I nor my brother liked what was going on. I was on the honor roll or principal's list for my grade point average for just about all the years in elementary school. The more I thought about what was going on at home, the more I lost interest in school. I let what was going on at home affect my school work. I did not have a problem with going to school; my mind was just consumed with what was happening between my parents. It is possible to lose interest in things you enjoy and excel at because of distractions.

One year, my grade point average dropped to a 1.9. This was because I wasn't putting enough time and effort into studying because my mind was focused on what was going on at home. Every kid wants their parents to have a great relationship because most kids look at their parents as an example of what they want their relationship to be like someday. You start to think to yourself, "Is this what love is really about?" All the going and coming back and all the "it won't happen again." On the outside, no one could tell what was going on with me, but on the inside, I was going through it. It was hurting so bad that there were a few times I opened up to one of my best friends, Deon, about it. He would always encourage me to stay strong. At a young age, I learned how to hide what I was actually feeling, which is not a good thing at all. Many people hide how they actually feel and what they are actually going through because they think it's the best thing to do. Well, it's not.

I didn't understand that hiding my emotions was a bad thing. I just did not want anyone to know what was going on at home and what I was feeling. People never get help or get better when they hold things in. Holding it in prevents you from dealing with it. We forget that we all need someone or something to help us get through what we are facing. I let what was going on at home affect what was going on at school. I needed to let out everything that I was feeling and all that was bottled up in me in a positive way. I found that playing sports is what allowed me to do so.

Releasing My Frustration

When it came to sports, track & field was my heart. I loved every second of it. It was something that I worked extremely hard at because I always wanted to be the best and I did not want anyone to be faster than me. In my elementary school, I was the fastest in my age group and I was probably top three in the entire school. At the time, I thought track & field was my passion. My school would have something called Sports Day. This was a day that the entire school would go to the track and field to compete against each other. There were about six or seven different groups and the school decided what group you were in. I always looked forward to this day because I loved to compete. Although I loved playing track & field, I also used it to let out my emotions about what was going on at home. It was a positive release for me. No one knew why I was so ready to compete. They just knew I was going to run hard. I used the crisis I was going through to help me in competition. Most people let what they go through force them into doing things on the negative side of the spectrum. I used it on the positive side. Running across that line in first place was a big relief to me. The entire time I was racing I would be thinking about what was going on at home and that would give me an extra boost. However, although I would win, I noticed that even after a win, it never changed how I felt about the situation. It still ate at me even after I had accomplished something good—even while doing something that I loved. I couldn't believe how much it was consuming my mind. When you see people you love who are hurting and struggling this tends to happen. I wanted desperately to help my parents, but I didn't know how.

My parents fighting and separating was one thing, but having a father who wasn't present at school or sporting events bothered me as well. My dad would never make it to any of my sports events. That bothered me so much. Looking in the crowd for him and watching other kids run to their dads after a race was very hard to deal with. My mom would attend every single thing that had to do with school and sports. I honestly can't remember a time that she wasn't there. That was another reason my mom and I were so close.

After sporting events, I remember my mom and I walking to the bus stop talking about my races and her telling me to keep working hard. I truly believe that young boys know that no matter what, moms are going to be there to support them. However, what every young boy wants is to be able to look up in the stands and see his father. There's something about a father-son relationship. A young boy yearns to look in the stands, see his dad, and make him proud. Although my dad was never there for anything, I still knew that he was very proud of me. This wasn't a situation where my dad didn't care, he did care about how I was doing in school and sports but he was just never there.

The reason my dad could never make it to any of the sporting and school events was because he was always working to provide for our family. He wanted to make sure we had everything we needed to do well in school and in sports. He may not have been at track events, but he was the one who made sure I had the uniform and shoes to compete. He may not have shown up to school events, but he was the one who made sure I had everything I needed for school. I knew these things but it still disappointed me that he was never there. Him not being there caused many people to think that my mom was a single parent, which obviously wasn't the case. I would lie down at night and say to myself, "Whenever I have kids, I am going to make sure I do the best I can to never miss an event that has to do with school or sports."

So there was this in-between feeling for me: I respected the fact that my dad worked so hard to make sure we had everything we needed but I still wanted him to be there for my sports event. This taught me that sometimes you don't get what you want, but you have to continue to deal with and be grateful for whatever you have. My dad had a tough life growing up, so he wanted to make sure we had all the things he didn't have when he was growing up. This caused him to miss a lot of things that he wished he could've attended but he was determined to not let us grow up the way he did. I respect and love him for that.

Moving On

When I was 8, we moved from the first house we lived in, on Meeting Street, to an apartment not too far away, on Lewis Street. This apartment was still in the hood, but it was better than the last one. I was happy when we moved to Lewis Street because a lot of people I knew lived in that area. A few of my cousins lived in that area as well, so that meant that I would be able to see them more often. Although this place was better than the first house, it was still small. We all still slept in the same bed, but we had a kitchen and a bathroom. We no longer had to take baths outside in a tin tub. That felt really good. My dad just kept working and working, so there was progress being made in the quality of my family's life. However, one of the scariest moments of my life happened in this house. One night my mom and my dad went to a club and left my brother and me home alone. They didn't leave my brother and me home alone very often, but on this night, I had to use the restroom really bad. When I got out of my bed to use go to the restroom, there was a guy standing in front of me. He reached into his pants and pulled out a gun. I went back to the bed and pulled the blanket over my brother's and my heads and held my brother tight. When we woke up, everything was all over the place. All our clothes were on the ground and all our drawers were open. The thief took our video game and all of my dad's money. He also took some of my mom's stuff as well. We were all heartbroken because we figured it had to be someone who knew us; someone who knew that my mom and dad would not be there or someone who actually watched my parents leave the house. This happened about two weeks before Christmas; the robber took all the money my dad had been saving up to make sure we had a great holiday. I replay this incident in my head many times I ask myself, "Why didn't he shoot me?" It took me over ten years to realize he did not shoot me because he could not see me. There was a reason he could not see me and I know that the good Lord had everything to do with it. I think a lot about how that night could have changed my whole life or even taken my life. The guy was close enough that if I had put my arms out, I could have touched him. I never told my parents that I saw the guy and he pulled out a gun. They don't know that happened. They won't find out until they read this book. We all have situations we have been faced with that our parents don't know about. For me, this is one of them.

As I said earlier, there was progress being made as far as our living conditions, but the fighting between my mom and dad continued. I would sit and cry, wondering if it would ever stop and why did it always happen? Then my mom would always leave. It was extremely frustrating for both my brother and me, but we had to live with it.

Living on Lewis Street was the first time I played basketball. My cousins, uncle, Demetrius, and friends who lived in the neighborhood were all good at it. I was a track guy, so basketball meant nothing to me. I remember one day my dad and I were walking from the bakery after getting some bread. We saw my cousins, Mikey and Donny, and some of my friends walking while bouncing a basketball. They said to my dad, "You should let Tum come play ball in the park with us sometime." In my mind I was thinking, "I'm not so sure about that." I had messed around with a basketball in the park where I used to live on Meeting Street but never was serious. I even remember my dad saying, "He don't play ball. He does track." Playing ball meant absolutely nothing to me because my goal was to be an Olympian. What meant absolutely nothing to me would soon mean everything to me. I had no idea that things were going to change, but they did and they changed really fast. Sometimes the things that don't mean much to us will become the things we fall in love with after spending some time with it.

After about a year and a half, we moved from Lewis Street to McKinney Drive, which was off of Carmichael Road. This was a very different environment. Lewis Street was in the hood, and McKinney Drive was not. Moving there was huge for us, but it was also hard. The reason it was hard for us was because we moved away from all the people we knew to living around people we had never met before. We moved from a place we were familiar with to go to a place that we were unfamiliar with. My brother and I had to make new friends, which is always hard to do because there is this fear of not knowing how people will receive you.

This time the living condition was the best it had ever been. For the first time, my brother and I shared a room, which meant that my mom and dad had their own room. Even though we finally had a room to ourselves, my brother and I still slept in the same bed. We had no problem with that at all. The apartment also had a living room, bathroom and a kitchen. It was really nice. Like I said earlier, my dad worked extremely hard to make sure we had the things that we needed. Even though the environment was much better, my mom and dad still fought and the results were the same. My mom would end up leaving the house and my brother and I would stay with my dad. Through this I realized that even in better environments, the same things can go on. I learned that changing environments really meant nothing unless you changed yourself.

We did not stay in that apartment long before moving again. However, we moved down the street to another apartment that was even bigger and better than the last one. At ten years old, this was the first time my brother and I had our own beds. My dad bought us twin beds. My parents had a room and my brother and I had a room. There was a kitchen and bathroom just like the other place, but this place was way better. Even though we had our own beds, some nights my brother and I still slept together. This apartment was great and my dad still lives there up until this very day.

Purpose Principles

1. Don't let the negative things you go through at home affect the positive areas of your life away from home.

2. Use what you go through to motivate you rather than keep you down.

3. Use the crisis you are facing as fuel to excel at other things.

4. Sometimes the things that don't mean much to you will become the things that you fall in love with.

5. Focus on accomplishing one thing at a time.

CHAPTER 4

First Time on the Court

"Sometimes what you start may not be the thing that you end up finishing."

I've always believed in the saying, "Finish what you start." I've learned that this saying holds true when you start something you love to do but quit because it gets too hard. Most people don't finish what they start because the journey to the destination is too painful and takes too much sacrifice. However, there are many times that you start doing something you love to do and plan on finishing it but stop doing it because you fall in love with something else. I am speaking directly from experience.

I never really played the game of basketball when I was growing up unless it was just for fun. I would go to the courts and mess around playing the game of 21. The first time I really played basketball I was about nine years old. I was at Hay Street Park with my cousins and friends and we were playing a full court game of basketball. I was super quick on my feet, so it was hard for anyone to stay in front of me and I could get by anybody whenever I wanted to. I enjoyed passing the ball to my teammates and working together with them to win the games. I had the time of my life and all of my friends told me how good I was. I went home saying to myself, "I had no idea I could really play." I remember thinking about that day and night. I realized it was just pick-up ball, but it felt amazing being a part of a team. Even with how good I was and all the praise from my friends and cousins, basketball would still be something I messed around with and played only for fun.

That changed when I got invited to play on the neighborhood team. I asked my parents if I could play and they said, "Yes." On my way to the first game, I was very nervous because I had never even practiced before. I thought to myself, "What if I don't play well?" I got to the game and one of the best players, who happened to be my cousin, wasn't there. When it was my turn to check into the game, it was like all my nervousness went away. The thought of me never practicing went away. I just went out and played. AND 1 Basketball was really popular at this time and my favorite move was crossing people over and making them fall. After the crossover, it was a must that I completed a pretty pass to one of my teammates. I was very flashy on the court. We won the game and afterwards they gave me my cousin's jersey number.

There were so many things going through my head after we won the game. The first thing I thought about was, "Man, this is not right I can't take my cousin's number." The second thing I said to myself was, "Wow, I can't believe they just did that." Then I started to think about how my cousin would feel about it and what would it do to our relationship. Surprisingly, it did not affect our relationship in a negative way. He was my older cousin, so he was proud of me. Him being proud of me helped me not to think about the situation negatively. What this taught me was that people will only use you based on how they need you. They needed me because my cousin was not there and, in turn, they gave me his jersey because he was not able to play. In all actuality, I may never have played if he was there so, in a sense, they used him too.

After that game, I played with the team as much as I possibly could but still did not practice basketball. We would walk to different neighborhoods to play other teams. As much as I enjoyed playing basketball, I had no idea that I loved the game. I would find out that I loved playing the game sooner than I thought though. One day, my team got together and walked to a neighborhood called Mason Addition to play their team. On the way to the game, the older guys were telling me that I had to show out because there was this kid on the other team who was the best in his area at our age. They were telling me how I could not let him outplay me. I was used to challenges because I ran track. I was thinking, "I don't care if he is the best in their area, I'm better than him." When we got there, they pointed him out. I said to myself, "I'm about to embarrass this guy." As usual, when I got in the game, I was all about the flashiness. Every time I got the ball, instead of focusing on winning the game, I was focusing on trying to make this kid look bad. I was not very successful at this and we ended up losing the game. I was hurt that we lost the game because I felt like it was my fault that we did. The older guys from the other team were saying, "We told you Tum is not better than him." This made me angry, so I asked to play the kid in a game of one-on-one in front of everyone. First one to score three points would win the game. He got the ball first because we were playing on their court. The first time he tried to score, he missed. I got the ball and scored. The next time I tried to score, I missed and he scored. All of the older guys were on the sideline yelling both of our names and telling us to not let the other score. It was very intense. The score is now tied 1-1 and I scored again to make it 2-1. All I needed was one point to win the game and because I was up 2-1, I started feeling myself. I missed the game winner and then the guy scored two baskets in a row. His older friends started going crazy and yelling, "We told you! We told you!" I shook his hand, walked off the court, and cried all the way back home.

I had never felt so defeated in my life. It was just a game of one-on-one, but I was so competitive and I wanted to win so bad that it did not sit well with me that I lost—especially losing in front of all of those people. It was embarrassing. This was when I realized that I loved basketball; I had never practiced for a game ever but I was so embarrassed about losing a game in front of people. In the game we lost, I went at that guy and I went at him in one-on-one but both times my pride got in the way and it cost me. I wasn't used to losing in competitions, so this taught me how deeply I cared about winning and it also motivated me to be the best I could be. One of the most important lessons I learned from this experience was that personal pride could get in the way of team success. At this time, I did not understand that you could be individually motivated in a way that could help your team. You can still accept an individual challenge in a team sport but do what you are supposed to do at a higher and more consistent level than your opponent, so you can win.

Accept the challenge, but don't hinder your team. Help your team. I did not go on the basketball court for a couple of days because I was ashamed. The talk in the neighborhood was how I lost and then went home crying like a baby. I thought to myself, "Why am I even crying over a sport that I really don't play or practice for?"

I had no idea at the time that what I started, which was track, may not be the thing I end up finishing.

Purpose Principles

1. Sometimes what you started may not be the thing you end up finishing.

2. Be aware that most of the time people will only use you based on how they need you.

3. Focusing on individual success more than team success can hurt the team.

4. Don't allow personal pride to hinder team success.

5. You can be individually motivated but it should be in a way that can help your team instead of hurt your team.

CHAPTER 5

I Love This Game

Track & field was everything to me and being an Olympian was something I always dreamed of. I worked extremely hard every single day to make that dream a reality. After my first game of basketball, I often had the urge to play every chance I got. There was this church called First Baptist Church. They had a basketball team. I did not attend the church but a lady who worked at my elementary school did. She asked me to join the team but, because I was still running track, she would tell me to make practices when I could, which wasn't very often. All the guys on the team were older than me and all of them were much better than me. We started playing in church league tournaments and if my schedule allowed, I made it to the games. I never really played in any of the games. At first I thought I never played because I did not make it to many practices, but I realized that I never really played because I was not good enough. The other guys were much better than me.

I remember being at a practice and I could not make a left-handed layup. I said to myself, "What am I doing?" Was I making a bad decision trying to play basketball? My mom never came to any of the tournaments I played in. She knew I liked playing basketball, but she didn't know how strongly I felt about it so she didn't come to the tournaments. She thought I was just doing it whenever I wasn't busy doing track.

Even though I was the youngest on the team and all the guys were better than me, I still felt like I should've played more. Sometimes I would get put in the game, but it would be the last 20 seconds. We played on outside courts, so after the games, I would put a little dirt on my shirt before I went home to make it look like I had played a lot. I felt so bad doing that, but I imagined I would have felt worse telling my parents that I don't even play five minutes in a game.

This taught me how to handle situations that didn't go the way I wanted them to without going to my parents and coaches involved. I lied to my mom about playing a lot, but I never once complained to the coach that she should be playing me more. I kept a great attitude and always cheered my teammates on in a win or loss. I was just grateful to be a part of the team. Besides, I knew that there was another sport I was much greater at than basketball. Don't run to your parents when things aren't going the way you think they should be going. Figure out how to make it work and understand that when you are playing a team sport, it's not just about you. I'm not encouraging you to lie like I did and pretend like you played a lot, but I am telling you not to run home to your parents all the time when things aren't going well. Now there will be some situations that only your parents can handle and should know about. But for the most part, most people don't even try to figure it out on their own. Getting parents and coaches involved can create tension between them that could really be avoided.

Track Scholarship

It was the morning of my sixth grade graduation as I was getting ready, I was nervous the entire time because I understood that graduations were a big deal. I was also nervous thinking about what and how many awards I would be taking home. You sit there and hear all your friends' names being called, looking back at your family in their seats while having some idea of what is going to happen and the awards you'll get. This day turned out to be one of the happiest days of my life. My name was called numerous times for awards that had to do with track and field. The biggest and best one of them all was when they called my name up to receive a track scholarship for a track club named Road Runners. I was very excited because this was a step in the right direction for me wanting to become an Olympian—following in the footsteps of my cousin, Nathaniel McKinney. This also meant that my parents did not have to come out of their pockets for me to do something that I loved.

Many times kids don't understand how much of a help it is to get a scholarship in something that they love doing. It takes an extreme amount of weight off of your parents' shoulders. A lot of parents can't afford to come out of their pockets but would love for their kids to play sports. So I encourage kids to work hard and put their best foot forward in trying to get scholarships, especially if your parents can't afford for you to play sports. I was ready for this next phase of my life but had no idea how quickly things would turn around.

After graduating from elementary school, I went to H.O. Nash Junior High School for grades 7 through 9. The first day of seventh grade, I remember taking an extra bag with me because immediately after school, I had to catch the bus to track practice. I was really looking forward to practice. It was more than I imagined it would be. Practice was very hard and very competitive but fun at the same time. There were so many kids who were faster than or just as fast as me so there was never a day that I did not have to compete. I knew that I could never take a day off. We would race up hills, which was something I had not done very often; trying to win while doing that was extremely hard. Racing uphill was uncomfortable every single day but track was something I was always comfortable in so I did it. Through this, I realized that as you get to higher levels in anything, the level of competition get higher too since you will be competing against people who are better than or as good as you. So you should never really let yourself get comfortable if you want to win. Bringing an extra bag to school on Monday, Wednesday and Friday became routine for me. However, on a day I did not have track practice, I would walk behind the school and watch the boys' basketball team practice. I would just sit there and watch—noticing how much fun they were having.

The first day I was watching basketball practice, I noticed that they struggled to do the three-man weave. They had to complete the drill for two minutes without dropping the ball and every man had to know where he should go in order to complete the task. The job could not be done if each player did not do what he was supposed to do and be where he was supposed to be—meaning that they needed each other in order for them to be successful. A pivotal lesson I learned that day was that there was no way for you to be successful individually. If your teammates are not doing their jobs and you aren't doing yours then the team will fail.

When I went back to track practice all I could think about was the basketball practice from the day before. We raced a lot in practice, constantly trying to get faster and beat the person next to each of us. I would win just about all of the races in practice and I noticed that I did not like the feeling of winning and celebrating by myself anymore. Catching the bus from track practice, still thinking about the three-man weave I saw at the basketball practice, I decided to take matters into my own hands.

The next time there was track practice I skipped it and went to the basketball practice. I wanted to be a part of what I saw that first day. The first time we did the three-man weave, guys were dropping the ball, not being in the right position and I was frustrated. It was not how I expected it to be. In life, things may not go the way you expect them to, but what do you do when that happens? Do you give up or do you remember why you started in the first place? I thought everything would go smoothly but watching from the sideline was much more different than actually playing the sport. I made it through the entire practice and I was very happy about that. On my way home after the first practice, I had no regrets about skipping track practice. I was actually glad I did. Even while being sore from defensive drills, I was still happy I went. Practice was frustrating, but I loved it enough to want to go back and get better. All I could think about was going to the next practice and how I would encourage all of the players to improve on the things we did not do so well. So I said to my-self, "I may not go back to track practice" and I didn't. I kept going to the basketball practice consistently and I made the team.

My parents had no idea that I was no longer going to track practice until one day my mom went to track practice looking for me. I was at basketball practice, of course. When I got home that day, she asked where I was and I told her that I had quit the track team to play basketball. You can imagine how angry my mom was,

listening to her son telling her that he had quit a scholarship to go play another sport. She wasn't happy with
me at all, but I fell in love with the game of basketball. I
fell so deeply in love that I started to break some rules.
When I would go to the park to play basketball, my
mom would tell me to be back home at a certain time.
I would stay so late past the time that she would have
to come to the park to get me. I would have to face the
consequences of breaking that curfew rule, but that did
not matter to me. It wasn't that I did not care about the
rules my mom made, I just fell in love with the game so
much that I couldn't think about anything else when
I was playing. My passion for the game was so strong
that I was willing to face any consequence that came
with it.

When I quit track without telling my parents, I learned
that sometimes it takes stepping out on a limb and
following your heart to do whatever it is that you want
to do. Sometimes following your heart may require
you not even telling your loved ones because it means
that much to you. You have to be willing to deal with
the consequences of the decisions you make and I was
willing to do that. Being on the basketball team taught
me how to be a part of something that would not only
benefit me or hurt me but would do the same for my
teammates. It showed me the beauty in coming together with a group of people for one common goal and,
on the road to achieving that goal, we would all need
each other. With track I did not need anyone for me to

be successful. With basketball, I had to count on other people every day. This also helped me to understand the saying, "Everybody needs somebody." That statement holds true not only in the game of basketball but in the game of life. I could not be successful without my teammates' help. Just like in life one cannot really succeed without the help of others.

I was a part of the team and we were working hard and getting better every day. We couldn't compete against schools that first year and this gave us time to learn our system better and how to play together as a team. The year went by pretty fast considering the fact that we weren't playing any games. It was a new year and a lot of guys came to try out, but we were already confident about who would make the team. The fact that we weren't able to play the year before because our team really wasn't that good gave us motivation and put a chip on our shoulders—not to mention our girls' team was the best around and had won at least 15 years in a row. Talk about pressure and motivation; We had both.

A day I will never forget is when the coaches picked the starting lineups. Hearing my name called to be the starting point guard was something I did not take for granted. I was a sprinter in track the year prior and now I was starting as point guard on the basketball team. The season started and we were playing really well. People were surprised and we took every game personally. Everyone assumed that we would not be good and then we made it all the way to the championship game. It took extreme focus and sacrifice to get there. School and basketball were the only things that mattered to us. We would not be able to get there if our minds were focused on other things. What helped me focus at such a young age was knowing that I had a chance to do something special. I understood in order to do that special thing, my focus could not be anywhere else. I had to give up so much of myself for the team in order to help us get to the championship. We had a very talented team with a lot of guys who could probably start on any of the teams we competed against, but all the guys bought in for the one common goal, which was to win a championship. There was no hanging out after school at the bus stop like the other kids. There was no going to parties on the weekends. Many Saturday mornings we were at practice from 8 am until about 11 am and sometimes we had practice twice a day. It was really hard to do at times, but we knew that if we wanted to accomplish something that hadn't been done in a long time, we had to sacrifice things that we wanted to do.

We won the championship and I had a feeling that words still can't explain. After winning, I sat back and thought to myself, "Quitting track was worth it." I would be lying if I said that I knew we would win a championship my first year of playing organized basketball, but it took so much faith to believe that something great was going to come out of the situation. In life, you may leave something you are really good at to do something that you can become great at. I promise if you just stick with it, it'll work out. The key is sticking with it. It won't work out if you give up as soon as it gets hard or as soon as it is not what you expected it to be. Be committed and trust the process.

Purpose Principles

1. How you handle situations that are not going the way you think they should or expect them to plays a huge role in determining the person you become.

2. Sometimes trying to follow in the footsteps of others can blind you to the fact that you may actually love something else.

3. In life, you need other people to be successful.

4. Sometimes following your heart requires you to take matters into your own hands, but you have to be willing to deal with the consequences of the decisions you make.

5. You may leave something you are good at to do something you can become great at. If you stick with it, it'll work out.

CHAPTER 6

Opportunity Knocks

"Sometimes the best things in your life happen when you least expect them to."

I t was just a normal day: my mom and I were at home, my dad wasn't there and I think my little brother was outside playing in the yard. We were in the living room watching television and suddenly there was a knock on the door. This knock sounded no different than any other knock before. However, it was a knock that would change my life.

I call it the knock of opportunity. There is a saying that goes, "opportunity is knocking at my door." On that particular day, it was. I went into the bathroom and my mom opened up the door. The guy at the door was someone everyone called Space but whose real name is Cedrick. I came out of the bathroom and he asked me, "Do you want to play basketball in America?" I said, "Yes. What do I have to do and where do I have to be?" I knew Space because his daughter was the best player on our girls' basketball team. He then told me that a coach from Florida would be having a basketball show-case at a high school and that he will be looking for players to take back to America to play. He said to be at the high school at 3 pm and I told him I would be there. I was very excited, but I was also extremely nervous.

There was absolutely no way I could sleep that night after hearing that there was a chance I could do what I love in America. There wasn't much opportunity back in The Bahamas for me to play the game at the level I wanted to. I thought to myself, "This could be a chance for me to play college basketball, go to the NBA, and move my family to America." This was a chance for me to play ball in "The Land of Opportunity"—something that was very rare where I'm from. I would be lying if I said I knew Space was coming to my house that day with that kind of news. I always wanted a chance to play in America. I just never knew if and when I would get the opportunity. I worked hard every single day without knowing what the outcome would be. I learned that if you stay persistent, control the things you can control and work hard every day, life can change for you when you least expect it. Being prepared for an opportunity without knowing when it will show up is what will help you achieve your dreams and goals. You will never know when that day is going to come so that is why it is important not to take breaks or try to figure out when things will happen. My job was to make sure I was ready for whenever the opportunity presented itself and it did that day.

Florida Workout

Saturday morning came very fast but I did not have to be at the high school until 3 pm. I sat at home nervous as could be, waiting on my aunt Racquel to pick me up. My aunt picked me up because neither of my parents had a car. On our way to the high school, I had no idea what to expect. For some reason when we got there my mom and aunt couldn't stay so they hugged and kissed me and told me to do my best.

I saw a few guys at the showcase that I knew and there were also many players there that I had never seen before. We went through some offensive and defensive drills then it was time for us to play. There were more older guys than younger guys at the showcase. The older guys took the court first as, we younger guys watched. There was a point guard there who was about four years older than me and he was very good. I had never seen him play before and he was so good that instead of watching the game I was watching him and trying to learn from him throughout the course of the game. He wasn't the fastest guy but he could get by his defender in one dribble. He was super crafty with the ball and could shoot the lights out of it. He reminded me a lot of Chris Paul. He would get by his defender in one dribble but he had a tendency to change directions and go the other way. There was no need for this player at the showcase to change directions because it just took him one dribble to get by his defender.

I sat on the sideline waiting to get in the game while I paid attention to everything that was going on. The point guard kept doing the same thing over and over, so the coach brought him in. He told him, "Stop changing directions. When you get by your defender let the big help and drop it off to your big so he can get a dunk." The coach was not talking to me, he was talking to the point guard about how to use the center, but I was listening to what was being said to him. The point guard went back in the game and did the same thing again, so the coach pointed at me and told me to go get the defender. I went in the game and, in the first play, I drove by my defender, the big helped, I dropped the ball off to my big and he got a dunk. That was the play that literally changed my life.

My ability to listen and apply something that wasn't being said to me allowed me to earn a scholarship to play in America. There is a saying in life that goes, "Experience is the best teacher." I don't believe that saying is 100% true. People choose to have experience the best teacher but sometimes it's better to not have the experience and learn from someone else's mistakes. Experience can cause you to lose opportunities, time and a lot of other things if that is the only way you learn something. I did not have to go on the court, get by my man and change directions to know that it wasn't what the coach wanted. I knew the coach didn't want me to do that because I was listening to him when he told the other point guard not to do it. Instead of experiencing what the point guard did, which ultimately led to him getting pulled out of the game, I learned from what he did, which resulted in me earning a scholarship. Often times, we think that a person has to be directly talking to us in order for us to listen, learn, and apply a message. I've learned that some of the most important principles you learn are the ones that are not being said to you directly but indirectly. That experience taught me the importance of listening and learning from others' mistakes, so I won't have to experience the things they do. Think about this for a minute: there was no way that my parents could afford for me to go to America but I got a scholarship because I was listening to something that was not even being said to me. Let that sink in. Are you paying attention to what's not being said to you? Sometimes what is not being said to you directly could be the thing that changes your life. I'm speaking from personal experience.

The showcase was over and the coach said he wanted me to be a part of the team. I could not believe it. Words can't express how happy I was, sitting down on the bench waiting for my mom and aunt to come and pick me up. When they got there, I smiled all the way to the car and told them that I got the scholarship. They were extremely happy for me. My aunt was so happy that she let me drive her car for a bit. We drove to West Street to give my dad the news. He was excited and proud of me. This was one of the best days of my life. I got the opportunity I wanted and it was time for me to take full advantage of it. Little did I know that I would have to wait before I could leave for The States.

Waiting on the I-20

It was now time for me to wait on my I-20 form, which is the form that I needed in order for me to go to school in America. This is a stage that no one who is trying to get to America enjoys. We all want what we want when we want it. This was a harsh process on top of the fact that my mom did not want me to leave because I was only 13. She kept saying, "You are not going" and my dad was like, "Let him go." It was hard for the both of them because I was their firstborn. Just imagine how my mom was feeling about me leaving—her firstborn whom the doctors told her she would never be able to have; the baby who almost killed her that she was not able to touch or see until he was four months old. This was very hard for my mom. But I had a burning desire to leave because I wanted to follow my dreams and move my family to America one day. So my mom finally agreed to let me go.

I would go onto the school's website every single day while I waited. It looked so nice. There was a pool on the homepage and next to it there was a guy in a cap and gown throwing his cap in the air. I thought to myself, "Man, this is going to be wonderful. I am going to have my own locker. I'm going to be in this nice school. I can't wait." When I would watch television and see schools in America, I would always see kids going to their lockers and wearing whatever they felt like to school. It was something I dreamt of doing as well. The schools I attended required that we wear school uniforms. We also didn't have lockers. Going to school in America was something I was really looking forward to.

As I was waiting on the I-20, I noticed that I was not getting any calls or communication from the coach. I started to worry. Was he selling me a dream? Was he lying to me about how good I was? Did I ever really have a chance at playing in America? Waiting already had me and my family anxious and then we were made aware of a hurricane watch. With hurricanes, you could never estimate what the damage would be if it actually occurred. It is a hard thing to deal with where I'm from because the island is so small. If a major hurricane were to hit our town, we would not know how to recover from the damage. Watching the damage of hurricanes in much bigger places always had us on edge. If a hurricane did that kind of damage in a town or country larger than ours, we couldn't imagine what it would do to ours. I prayed every day that the coach would not send the I-20 at the same time the hurricane watch was going on. If the hurricane did hit, I knew the airport would be shut down, which meant I would not be able to go to America. I was nervous and scared every day because nothing was going the way it was supposed to go or the way I thought it was supposed to go.

I remember walking in my dad's room one night and he could tell that I was down about the whole situation. My dad said to me, "He will call, Tum. He will call. Just be patient." Within the next couple of days I received a phone call from the coach saying that the I-20 was finished and was on its way. I think the showcase was in June and I did not get the I-20 until September so you can see why I thought I was being sold a dream. I was so excited when I got the scholarship that if it was up to me, I would have left the day after. Waiting on the I-20 taught me how to be patient in the midst of not under-standing what is really going on. I was about to follow my dreams, but it still was not an easy decision for me to make, especially because of my younger brother. My brother and I were very close growing up and still are to this very day. I never knew what it felt like to not be around him. We were together all the time and I knew deep down in my heart that this was going to be tough for the both of us. He was 11 years old at the time— only two years younger than me. I'm not sure if my little brother knows this, but he is a huge reason I am who I am today. He followed me so much when we were growing up that it forced me to do the right thing as much as I could. I'm not perfect, no one is, but knowing he was always watching me helped me to make good decisions. I wanted him to succeed, so I had to make sure I was a great example for him. Thank you, Laquan. I wouldn't be who I am today without you.

October 2, 2008. I was in a car headed to the airport to start a journey that would change my life forever. So many different emotions were going through me all at the same time. There were a lot of firsts for me: I had never been away from my family before for any amount of time—other than the times when my mom and dad would split up, we were always together; I had never been to America before; and I had never been on an airplane before. But I had to do things I had never done before, to get to a place I had never been before. Are you willing to do that? In that car ride, tears ran down my face because I had an extreme appreciation for my family. I always appreciate my family, but knowing that I would not be able to see them whenever I wanted to broke my heart. Knowing that I would wake up the next day and not see my brother, my mom or my dad, was mind-boggling to me, but I had a dream in my heart that I had to make a lot of sacrifices for. I had to pay a price and although it hurt badly and cut deeply, I had to do it. Getting on the airplane with so much on my mind, I started to panic because I had never flown before. I did not know what to expect. I was very afraid until I realized that I had absolutely no control of the airplane. That thought made me calm down a little because I understood that I did not have to be afraid in a situation I had no control over.

Purpose Principles

1. Sometimes the best things in your life happen when you least expect them to.

2. Stay persistent and control what you can because you never know when opportunity will knock on your door.

3. Listening to what is being said to you indirectly may have a bigger impact on you than what is being said to you directly.

4. Experience doesn't have to be the best teacher; it only becomes the best teacher if you refuse to learn vicariously from someone else's mistakes.

5. Following your dreams comes with a price.

CHAPTER 7

Something Ain't Right

"What do you do when the opportunity doesn't look like you thought it would?"

As I walked out of the airport in Ft. Lauderdale, Florida, I looked around and was in awe of how big the place was. It was an extreme culture shock for me. The coach picked me up and on the ride from the airport I stared out the window the entire time, amazed at how big everything was. There were so many huge buildings, signs and nice cars that I had only seen on TV before. I was very quiet on the ride not because I was afraid but because I was so thankful to be there. Excitement ran through my body and I still get the chills to this very day thinking about how grateful I was for the opportunity. It took us about fifteen minutes to get to our destination but because of all the emotions, it felt like the longest ride of my life.

We pulled into a strip mall and parked. At the end of the strip mall were a few restaurants, but I didn't see a pool. I didn't see any big beautiful trees and I didn't see happy students dressed in their own clothes either. "What is going on?" I thought to myself. I looked out at the strip mall and I saw a building. There was no way possible this was the school. Three or four rooms on the second floor of that building turned out to be our entire school. It didn't look anything like the website. I was confused, excited and grateful all at the same time. It wasn't what I was expecting, but I knew I had to make it work.

Shortly after we arrived, I was told to pack a little bag because we were going out of town. I packed my basketball shoes and shorts. I was ready to play some ball. I got very excited because I thought we were going on a road trip to hoop. I felt big-time and started feeling myself—that was until we drove seven hours to Tallahassee, Florida, and arrived at a Bethune Cookman and FAMU football game. When we got there, coach grabbed some tables and set them up so we could sell t-shirts at the game. Once again, a feeling of confusion came upon me. We started selling the t-shirts to people going in and out of the game. It was already awkward selling the shirts and to make matters worse I didn't know any of the other players so we weren't really talking. We were all from Nassau but we didn't know each other so we didn't talk to each other. Looking back, I think everyone was confused about what was going on. Despite the confusion, none of us complained because it was a chance for us to put money in our pockets. Everything looked absolutely different than how I saw it in my head. I learned right then and there that things can turn out to be the total opposite of what you thought they were going to be.

The First Night

I could not believe I was at a football game selling t-shirts instead of playing basketball. The coach never explained to us why we were selling t-shirt, but he did give each of us a portion of the money we made. We never questioned him either because we saw selling the shirts as a way to make some money. All the guys who went on the trip now had some extra money. After selling the shirt, we headed back to Ft. Lauderdale no questions asked. When we arrived back, we pulled up to the house where we were staying in. There were twenty-one of us staying in a three-bedroom house with one bathroom. Well, really we had two bathrooms and two bedrooms. One of the bathrooms was the coach's and the other one was ours. I sat in my room on the bunk bed wondering what I had gotten myself into. I was nervous, confused and scared, but I still had that dream in my heart. I was the youngest one in the house, so I had to stand my ground and believe in myself amongst a group of guys who were older than me. There were so many guys there and I didn't know even one of them, so I stayed to myself.

The first night in the house was brutal for me and it wasn't because I was living in a house with so many people. I already knew I would be able to adjust to that. It was brutal for me because I wanted to go back home. This whole experience was going nothing like I thought it would. We had to stand in line to get food because there were so many of us. I lay in bed that night with tears running down my face, thinking about my family. I was trying to figure out how I was going to make it in this situation. I cried the entire night until I fell asleep for what felt like only an hour. I woke up to a knock on the door at about 4:30 am. Coach told us that we had twenty seconds to get our shoes on and get outside. I rushed to get my shoes on while trying to figure out what could we possibly be doing this early in the morning.

This would be day one of conditioning for me. We ran about three and a half miles while the coach followed us in his car. While we were running, my focus was on not ending up in the back and following the guys who knew where we were going. I hated waking up at 4 am, but it instilled in me the discipline to get up early and do something productive before most people got their day started. I couldn't understand how important that was at thirteen years old because I felt like we should not have been up that early in the first place, but now it makes so much sense to me. I was in the middle of something I had never experienced before and whether I liked it or not, I had to embrace it. The truth is that it was making me a better person.

When we got back to the house I could barely feel my legs. I ran cross country a couple times before but it was never at 4:30 am without stretching. We all had to say who was using the bathroom first, second, third and so on. If you weren't using the bathroom, you were eating breakfast. That first morning after coming back from running, I ate a bowl of Cap'n Crunch cereal. I had to eat it fast, knowing it would soon be my turn to shower and, because there were so many of us, we all had only two minutes to be in the bathroom. After showering, we all had to get ready for school and then head to the bus. I was still excited for the first day of school despite it not being the way it looked on the website.

The first day of school was just like any other first day of school. We had to stand up in class, introduce ourselves and say where we were from. Even though I was excited about school, I was really looking forward to seeing where we would practice. After school, half of us got on the bus to go to practice while the other half waited. The bus couldn't fit us all at once. I was excited on the bus—excited to see where we were going to practice. We pulled up to a recreational center. I thought we were going in the gym, but I was wrong. We practiced on the courts outside. Practice was extremely hard. We started off by running about two miles. We ran before practice, during practice and after practice. Because I was the youngest and wanted to prove myself, I tried my hardest to never lose a sprint and always do the drills harder than everyone else. The amount of running we had to do didn't make any sense to me. After practice my entire body was sore, but, in that practice, I learned that I could push myself beyond my own expectations.

I could not believe everything that I had experienced so far: first day going to sell t-shirts at a football game; coming back to sleep in a three-bedroom house with twenty other guys; waking up at 4:30 am to run three and a half miles; going to school on top of a strip mall; and then practicing outside. I started to tell myself that I had to go back home, but I still had that burning desire in my heart to play college basketball, go to the NBA and move my family to America. Those weren't the only things keeping me in America. I didn't think I was good enough yet; if I would have left The States, I didn't think I was good enough yet to get another opportunity to come back to America. So I stayed. I promised myself I would work as hard as I could to get better at the game and to get more people to notice my talent. I figured that would be the only way I would get another opportunity.

The entire school situation continued to become harder and harder and guys started to quit. They started to leave and go back home. This was hard to watch because just like them, I wanted to leave too. Going through this experience helped me to realize how badly I wanted to achieve my goals. I was determined to make this situation work regardless and, like I said earlier, I was not good enough to leave. Most younger guys follow the lead of guys who are older than them. I believe that statement to be very true. However, in my case, it wasn't. In this particular situation, I wasn't going to follow the lead of anyone but myself and I didn't.

Being at the school was extremely tough; I knew on the first day that something was wrong. Was this the price I was supposed to pay in order to turn my dreams into a reality? At one point, I started to think it would be too hard for me to deal with. Back in The Bahamas, whenever I would dream of something, I would only believe those things could come true in my dreams. In other words, the things that I saw myself doing when I closed my eyes, I believed could only happen when I closed my eyes. I thought that it would be different because I made it to the land of opportunity, but what I had experienced so far made me think otherwise. I started to have doubts. What if those were only dreams? What if my dreams are really too hard to achieve? Maybe my dreams can actually only happen in my dreams. Can I ever make them a reality? About a week later, a new guy showed up from Nassau whose name was Jahman Delancy. We were the same age; we were born about two weeks apart. I stayed to myself when I first arrived at school, but when Jahman showed up, he instantly became my best friend. We shared things in common besides the month we were born. We both had the same desires of wanting to make it for our families and take care of them one day. Also, I think the fact that we were both so young also made us close. We would push each other extremely hard every day and would always look out for each other. Having him there with me made things a little bit easier. Just a little bit.

Purpose Principles

1. Most of the time, the opportunities we get won't look like what we expected them to.

2. How you respond when things don't look the way you thought they would is very critical to becoming successful in life.

3. When you ask yourself, "What did I get myself into?" you are on the road to success.

4. Getting up early in the morning gives you the opportunity to get better before most people get their day started.

5. The journey will always make you second guess whether you can actually turn your dreams into reality.

CHAPTER 8

First Time for Everything

"Doing it on your own speeds up maturing process."

B ack home in The Bahamas, my mom and dad took care of almost everything for me: grocery shopping, school shopping, cooking and most of the cleaning. The only thing I was really responsible for was ironing my school uniform. I had it easy in terms of having responsibility growing up. Being in America alone, I would see how difficult taking care of myself and being responsible was.

I remember the first time I went to Walmart to get things for myself. I always watched my mom and dad make a list of things they needed from the store before they went so I did the same exact thing. The first time I walked in Walmart it was so huge; I couldn't believe it. I thought that this store had everything anyone could ever need. Back home, we did not have a store that was even close to being the size of Walmart so I thought it was pretty amazing.

This was my first experience shopping for myself. School uniform, snacks, juices and my school supplies were some of the things I got. I felt like I was older than I actually was. We spent about two hours shopping because the store was so big and I kept seeing things I wanted. I got a lot of things that day, but I really did not spend a lot of money. Some of the prices blew my mind. I was used to buying a bottle of Gatorade back home for $2 and I could get about eight of those at Walmart for $4. The price for everything was so much cheaper in America and it made me realize why people from back home always came to America to shop—because it saved them money.

My cousin, Mikey's, best friend, Ray, was at the school with me. After the first time at Walmart, whenever we would go again, he and I would share a cart. We would push the cart all around the store and put the things we both wanted in there. Afterwards, when it was time to pay, we would split the bill half and half. Every time I ran out of things I needed, I went to Walmart. It started to become easier to shop. I was used to my parents doing my shopping, but, now, I was doing it on my own and it felt good.

I think that many kids struggle when they get older because they are so used to their parents doing everything for them. My being able to shop on my own was a big part of my maturing process. It became something I had to do not something I wanted to do. Being on my own meant that if I did not shop for myself nobody else would. This experience made me comfortable about doing things on my own. There came a time where a list was no longer needed before going to the store because once I ran out of things, I knew what I had to get.

Miami Dolphins Games

My time in Florida was made up of a lot of first-time experiences—things that I had never done before and hadn't really thought about doing like shopping for myself, selling t-shirts at football games and waking up early in the morning to workout. These experiences taught me that doing things you've never done before will bring out certain traits that you never knew you had inside of you. I was not comfortable doing any of those things the first time I did them, but that changed over time.

One of the most uncomfortable times at school was the first time I sold t-shirts at a Miami Dolphins football game. I had already sold t-shirts at football games before, but this time it was different. I grew up being a Miami Dolphins fan because my dad told me when I was a baby he used to dress me in Miami Dolphins gear. Never in my life did I believe I would be selling t-shirts at one of their games though. I always imagined going to a game someday and I did—just not in the way I expected to go.

We woke up one morning and it was our job to pack up the shirts and put them in the car. So here I am packing the Miami shirts in the car from size small all the way up to XXL. Driving on the way to the game, I knew we were going to sell the shirts, but I was still excited to see the stadium. When we arrived, we went to one of the parking lots. I grabbed a duffle bag, filled it up with shirts in all the sizes. I placed the bag over my head and on my shoulders, held one of the t-shirts in my hand for display and started to sell them. When we sold shirts in the past, I was able to sit down because the shirts were displayed on a table. However, this was more embarrassing because we had no table, so I had to walk around to people and try to sell the shirts rather than have people come to the table.

"Dolphins t-shirts five dollars! Get your Dolphins t-shirts." The parking lot was huge and there were a lot of people. I was very uncomfortable. What embarrassed me the most was when people flipped me off. I would walk up to someone's tent, ask them if they wanted to buy a shirt and I'd get the finger. Being rejected hurt my feelings because I was just a kid. It was in those moments that I realized that I wasn't being rejected because I was a kid though. Rejection does not care how old you are or what you look like, so it was my job to keep doing what I came to do and not let my feelings get in the way. I could not stop selling the shirts just because someone told me they did not want to buy it. I had to move to the next person no matter how I felt.

At this time in my life, I didn't understand that God was preparing me to deal with rejection. I now know that God was teaching me how to deal with rejection and keep going despite the obstacles. Most people stop at the place where they have been rejected. It's important to understand that you are supposed to keep pushing past the rejection. What comes after rejection is very sweet. I noticed that when I moved to the next person after being rejected, I would sometimes end up selling more than one t-shirt to that person. My team and I continued going to the games and selling t-shirts. Because of that, I made a lot of friends and became known around Florida. Sometimes, I would see some of my friends while I was selling t-shirts and, because I was embarrassed, I would hide. Selling t-shirts became familiar to me and I became good at it, but, at the same time, I was always afraid. We did not have a license to sell t-shirts at the games, so this made it illegal and dangerous. Some of my teammates got caught selling t-shirts and put in handcuffs by the police. Whenever I saw the cops, I would take off my duffle bag, put it under a car, hide and remember where I put it. I did not want to be put in cuffs.

We were going to the games so much that I started trying to figure out how to make even more money. I decided to start selling t-shirts for the visiting teams also. I would sell those t-shirts too because their fans would buy the shirts very fast. I made more money doing this. Even though we were making money, selling t-shirts took a lot out of me and my teammates. We were on our feet all day walking around in 90 degree weather. Not to mention that on some of those days we would practice, making it even worse.

First Christmas Break
My parents would call me all the time and ask me how things were going. I would tell them things were good. Obviously, I was lying because things weren't going good at all. I hated being there, but I was not ready to leave yet.

I went home for Christmas break and I was so excited to see my family and friends. I felt like I had become a different person since leaving and I was anxious to see if being back home would feel different also. The entire plane ride, I sat there smiling and thinking about the expression that would be on my mom, dad and little brother's faces. I got home and opened the door. My dad was sitting in the living room and when I walked in he told me I looked bigger and taller, all with a huge smile on his face. My mom and brother came into the living room and hugged me so tight. They were so excited to see me and told me how much they missed me. It had only been about two months since I had left, but it always feels like forever when you are away from the people you love.

The next day, I went to see more people in my family and they were all just as excited to see me. Seeing some of my old classmates, they all told me how proud they were of me. They encouraged me to keep doing what I was doing and let me know that I was inspiring many people. My entire family was especially happy. Even though my brother and I had everything we wanted and needed growing up, my family always struggled; my father always did what he needed to in order to provide for us, but working a lot was hard on him. Actually, all of my family struggled to make ends meet. Because life was a struggle, me getting the opportunity I did and going to America, gave everyone in my family a sense of pride. My grandmother would tell me how much she always bragged about me at her job. It made me realize that I had to keep persevering and stay in Florida. There was no way I could come back home, no matter how hard it got. Everyone in my neighborhood and my family was being impacted by what I was doing. I realized how much of a positive impact I had on them.

Being back home helped me to remember why I had left in the first place and it was a big part of making me want to work so much harder when I got back to school. Seeing my mom, dad and brother was weird for me the first few days. I went from seeing them every day of my life to not seeing them at all for about two months. Waking up and not seeing them started to become normal for me. It made my first morning back home extremely special. During my break, my brother and I cherished all the time we had together. We talked a lot about how different things were for the both of us now that I was living in America.

The day came for me to leave again and this time I was even more excited. I wasn't excited about going back to the school; I didn't actually want to go back there at all, but seeing everyone's reactions and knowing how proud they were of me made me want to keep up the hard work I was putting in. Despite how I felt, I still had a dream to fulfill. That visit home took my dedication, discipline and determination to a whole different level.

Purpose Principles

1. Doing it on your own speeds up the maturing process.

2. If you don't do what you have to do for yourself, no one else will.

3. When you do something you haven't done before you discover things you never knew you had inside of you.

4. Rejection does not care how old you are or what you look like.

5. Never stop because you experience rejection.

CHAPTER 9

More Motivation

Knowing that I would see my family and friends again when I went home for Christmas break motivated me. When I returned to school, I returned with a laser focus. I paid attention more in class, lifted harder in the weight room, ran harder in sprints and played harder on the court. I took everything to another dimension because I saw how much of a positive impact I had on everyone back home. One of my teammates, Demetri, used to wake me up at 5 am on our off days, so we could workout. I never had an issue with getting up but I just couldn't understand why he would only wake me up out of everyone else in the house.

Our workouts would consist of using stretch bands to do curls and Demetri made me do lots of pushups. God will always place people in your life who see more in you than you see in yourself. Demetri saw something in me that I did not see in myself. Sometimes in life you may not understand why certain things happen or why certain people are in your life, but, after a while, it becomes clear and makes complete sense to you. It started making sense to me when Demetri no longer had to wake me up in the morning; I started to get up on my own. That was a game changer. I was no longer doing it because Demetri wanted me to; I was doing it because I wanted to.

Same Environment, Different Focus

The situation at school didn't change; I was in the same environment, but I now had a different mindset. I stopped focusing on how much I hated the school and I started going harder, so I could leave. Going back home to visit and knowing that people were inspired by me taught me how to focus on the bigger picture and not on what was actually going on in front of me. Instead of worrying about having to practice outside, I focused on making every practice the best one it could be. Instead of worrying about having to run sprints, I focused on winning every one of them. Instead of worrying about selling t-shirts, I focused on seeing if I could sell the most shirts. None of this made my time there easier, however, it made me work harder to leave.

During the school year, my teammates, coach and I moved to a different house. There were about twenty-three of us total in this house. The new house was almost the same as far as the number of rooms and bathrooms. There were three bedrooms and two bathrooms; the coach had his bathroom and we had ours.

We were used to sharing one bathroom. but this one was different. Because there were more of us taking showers, the tub clogged up. Just imagine twenty plus guys taking a shower and the dirty water staying in the tub and almost reaching up to our calves. The water was so dark because it was filled with dirt. I had to put my feet in that water to shower and ended up getting a couple calluses, which were very painful, on the bottom of my toes. I had to get them removed because they hurt so bad when I played ball.

My dad came from The Bahamas to visit me once. I was hesitant for him to come because I knew he would not agree with how many of us were living together. I spoke with my dad about that visit and he recalls walking in the house and all he could smell was foot odor. He remembered seeing how many of us were staying in the same house and noticed that the coach sold snacks to us. One of my teammates actually bought my dad a Snickers bar from the coach. I'll never forget my dad pulling me inside my room, shutting the door and asking if I wanted to go home, like any parent would in this situation. He did not like what he saw.

I looked my dad straight in his eyes and said, "No, I'm staying. I'm going to thug it out." It was nothing against my dad. He reacted how any father would. Honestly, I'm sure some parents would have forced their child to go home with them. I knew my dad wanted me to go home and no offense to my dad but he did not have the dream, I did. I believed and wanted to turn my dreams into a reality so bad that I told my father I wasn't going anywhere. Do you believe in your dreams enough to look a loved one in the eyes and say, "I'm going to make it work"?

Where I lived was bad, maybe even terrible, but I was determined to make it work. In order to be successful, you have to make your situation work. It's not an option; it's a requirement.

Things Get Harder

Being in a different house was not the only thing that changed. We also changed our school to another location. As a matter-of-fact, we changed school locations five different times in total. This particular location happened to be right across the street from the strip mall. Before we changed locations each time, we did a lot of work on the building we were going to. All the building needed a lot of repairs and a team of twenty-three guys was cheap labor, so we always worked. Our days would start with us waking up early in the morning to go get breakfast from McDonald's. After breakfast, we would head to the school to break some walls down. After tearing them down, we would then have to build new walls. After building the walls, we would have to paint them. Every single one of us hated doing the work. We would talk about how it did not make any sense because we came to play basketball. The manual labor, selling t-shirts at Dolphins games and practicing outside—none of it was what we expected. Plus we each had to pay $300 a month for housing. With all of the work we were doing and the conditions we lived in, we should have been the ones getting paid $300 a month instead. The coach even started making us stand at red lights and beg for money. We had to say, "Excuse me, could you sponsor us for our basketball team, please?" We would do this for hours at a time. Some people would stop, but most would keep going and flip us off. Just like selling t-shirts at the Dolphins games, after being rejected, I had to keep going. There were so many times I was tempted to steal some of the money I made, but my heart would not let me do it.

We were doing so much work that I thought I had a job. Across the street from the strip mall wasn't the only placed we moved to. We changed locations at least four times in year but we were never told why he had to move so much. We were also the ones moving everything. Whenever we moved, we would rent a U-Haul and move all the desks and chairs out of the current building to whatever building we were going to. At one of the buildings, we had to buff the floors before putting the chairs and desks down. Practice was already hard and working before practice did not make it any easier. To make matters worse, some days we practiced in a gym, but most days practice was outside in the heat.

The longer I was there, the harder it became to stay.

Daily, I thought about telling my parents what was happening, but I knew they would make me come home, so I had to pay the price that came with not telling them the truth. The good thing was that my game was getting better. More people started to know who I was because I was now in the 8th grade starting on varsity. I was ranked as a top ten point guard in the country and the number two player overall in the state of Florida for my age group. I continued to work as hard as I could on and off the court and was starting to see the results. My roommate, Jahman, and I started staying up late at night talking about when and how we were going to leave the school. I wanted to leave so bad that I started to text a coach from another school, of course without telling my coach. But him not knowing would change very fast.

We were not allowed to take our phones to school, but I very seldom followed that rule. One day, throughout the school day, I was texting the coach from the next school; we were talking about me leaving the school I was at. My coach would pick some of us up after school and I was one of them. I knew he was about to pick me up and normally I would delete the texts between me and the other coach before being picked up, just in case I left my phone laying around somewhere. On the way home, I was riding in the front seat and I got a text from the new coach. Not even thinking, I pulled my phone out of my pocket and while I was reading the text, my coach asked me why I took my phone to school. I wasn't even thinking straight at that moment because, if I had been, I would have waited until I got home to look at the text. Next thing I knew, my coach snatched my phone out of my hand and looked at the messages between me and the other coach. He was not happy at all. He asked me if I wanted to leave, but the tone he used wasn't a friendly one.

As a teenager I had never been in a position like this before so I did not know what to do. I did what I had learned to do while I was there—I lied my way out of the situation. I was already used to lying because I lied to my parents all the time about how everything was going at school. So lying to the coach was not a big deal. When this happened, it put a strain on my relationship with my coach, but I honestly didn't care. I'm not saying that lying is a good thing, but I had done it so much before that it was easy for me to do again. This shows how whatever you practice, you will eventually perform, whether it is something good or bad.

The basketball season continued and I continued to get better. More people started to notice me. An assistant coach from Florida Atlantic University came to one of my practices. Even though I was extremely humbled and excited for the opportunity to have him watch me practice, I was also embarrassed. This was the first coach to come to one of my practices and he had to come watch me on an outside court. We could not even get a gym that day. I will never forget that feeling as long as I live. I see him now, standing up watching me practice. Despite that, my first college visit was an unofficial visit to Florida Atlantic University and it was an amazing feeling. I remember sitting down at the practice, soaking it all in and meeting Coach Mike Jarvis who was the head coach at that time. That visit made me want to work harder. Stopping was not an option. I wanted more and I wanted to be better. My journey at this point made me realize that success would come if I continued to work through whatever I was going through and did not give up. I also figured out that I could either get comfortable with success that I had already achieved or I could become hungry for more success. I wasn't comfortable with what I had accomplished. I wanted to be successful on another level and in my mind this was just the beginning for me.

Purpose Principles

1. Don't focus so much on how much you hate what you are going through; instead, use that energy to change what you are going through.

2. Learn how to focus on the bigger picture and not what is actually going on.

3. When you can look a loved one in the eyes and tell them you are going to make whatever you are going through work, you are on the road to turning your dreams into reality.

4. In order to be successful, you have to make whatever "IT" is, work.

5. Success can make you complacent or it can make you more committed.

CHAPTER 10

Decision Time

"I don't care what they think."

Now I'm in the ninth grade, known around the country and very well-known in the state of Florida. I was not the same player I was when I first left home at thirteen years old. I had been in America since thirteen and I was now sixteen. Even though I was getting better as a player, I wanted to go home and, at the same time, I didn't want to go home. I was stressed out. The thought of leaving America and going back to The Bahamas was weighing on me so heavily that I started to lose sleep at night. I still never mentioned to my parents that I actually wanted to come home. I still told them everything was good every time they asked. My parents trusted me, so they took my word for it.

The school conditions were so bad that some of my teammates started to leave for good, which made me staying become even harder. There were a few times I wanted to leave with some of the guys, but I just couldn't do it yet. Something kept telling me that it was not the right time. The season was still going on and I was having a great year on the court. My game was more mature because I understood the game much more than I did when I first came. We call this basketball IQ and if your IQ is high, you're a more valuable player.

Although initially I didn't leave when I first wanted to because I felt like I was not good enough to get another opportunity, that was not the case anymore. I was very confident in myself and my game. I knew that if I left I would get another chance to come back. Still I struggled with actually leaving and now it was because I was afraid of what people back home would say. Would I be looked at as a failure? Would they think I wasn't tough enough? Would they say I wasn't good enough? Would they think I gave up? The thought that bothered me the most was thinking that if I went back, my parents would be embarrassed—not so much my dad because he does not care what people say in general, but I knew my mom would not like me leaving the school. I fought back and forth with myself for about two months, trying to make the right decision. After many sleepless nights, I came to the conclusion that I shouldn't worry about what other people have to say about me making a decision for my life. I think that always leads to failure.

I had to get over worrying about what people would think of me for leaving the school and doing what I believed was best for me. Was it hard? Of course it was. But at the end of the day, I had to live with the consequences of the decisions I made, nobody else. My parents didn't, my friends didn't and just people in general didn't. Through this process, I learned that you have to make a decision that you feel is best for you despite what other people might think. Worrying about other people's opinions is one of the biggest ingredients to not making it where you want to go in life. The people you are worried about are living their lives happily while you are stressing about what you think they are thinking about you. I had to get over that and I did.

It was Christmas break of my freshmen year of high school and my mind was already made up that once I went home, I was not going back to the school. Instead of packing up all of my things, I just took a normal size bag of clothes, which made it look like I was coming back to Florida. No one would leave all of their clothes behind if they knew they weren't coming back. Everyone would know I didn't plan on coming back if I had taken all my clothes. I wanted to leave so bad that the rest of my clothes did not matter to me. I figured I could buy more or just come back and get them one day. I flew back home knowing that I was not going back. Explaining why I left school to my parents was still the biggest hurdle I had to jump. The plane landed and I was back at home. I put on a front like everything was normal; the whole entire time I was thinking about how I'm going to tell my parents that I was not going back to the school and what their reactions would be. I had also been lying to them and now I had to come clean about what was going on at school. That wouldn't sit too well with them either.

It was the day before we had to report back to school and I still did not say a word to my parents about me not wanting to go back. I was so afraid because I did not know what the outcome would be. That whole day was hard for me, but I acted normal. I didn't even tell my little brother I wanted to leave the school. It was a secret I kept from my entire family. The day I was supposed to return to Florida came. I went around the neighborhood to say goodbye to family and friends, packed all of my bags and then it was time to go. I remember it like it was yesterday. My mom told me to get in the shower because my ride was on the way to take me to the airport. I went in the bathroom, locked the door and stared in the mirror. The whole time, all I could think about was everything I had been through at the school from the time I arrived at thirteen years old to now at sixteen years old. Tears started to run down my face. I knew I couldn't do it anymore. I could not keep lying to my parents. I had to tell them the truth.

My mom started to bang on the door, yelling at me to hurry up and get out of the shower. I was on the ground crying. I had one of those moments that everyone is going to have in life if they haven't already. It is that moment when you look at yourself in the mirror and ask, "Do you really want to keep doing this?"

My mom told me to open up the door and before I did, I wiped my face. I opened the door and she started to yell at me. "Why haven't you showered yet? Your ride is on the way!" With tears in my eyes, I looked at her and told her I wasn't going back. She was confused, wondering why I would say something like that. "You are going back. Now get ready."

"No, I am not," I replied.

My dad jumped in and said if I didn't want to go back then I didn't have to. My mom was furious and she couldn't believe it. I then came out and told her about everything: the lies, selling t-shirts, begging on the streets, the manual labor and practicing outside. I told my parents everything. They were furious—my dad more than my mom—after hearing about what I experienced for the last three years. It was a "wow moment" for both of them. They asked me how I could keep all of that from them for so long. I told them I had to do what I had to do in order to get better at the game and put myself in a position for a better opportunity.

Even after telling them all the bad stuff, it was still hard for me to actually stay home. I knew my mom would be hurt and not want me to say at home, but at the end of the day, I had to do what was best for Tum. I would have to live with the final decision of me not going back, not my family. Being back at the school would hinder me from getting to where I wanted to go, so I followed my heart and left the school in Florida.

Are you willing to follow your heart to get to where you want to go in life? It was painful to go against what everyone else thought I should do, but everyone else did not have my dream, I did. I got to a point where what others thought about me or what they wanted me to do didn't matter anymore. What mattered was what I believed and wanted. This experience taught me how to express what bothers me sooner than later. The longer you wait to let go of things that bother you, the more they will weigh you down. It doesn't matter what people think about you or what they may think about the decisions you make. Follow your heart. Stop worrying about what other people think about you.

Purpose Principles

1. Worrying about what others say about you will keep you from your destiny.

2. You have to live with the consequences of the decisions you make.

3. Not making a decision you feel is best for you because of what other people may say is one of the biggest ingredients to not making it where you want to go in life.

4. Following your heart can be painful but worth it.

5. The longer you wait to let go of things that bother you, the more they will weigh you down.

PART III: DIVINE ORDER

CHAPTER 11

Home Again

There was a lot on my mind after I decided to stay home, but I knew I did what was best. Every day, I asked myself if I would ever make it back to America. I was extremely excited about being home after being away for three years. Although I was excited about that, I was frustrated that I was not doing what I loved in America. Frustration and happiness wrapped together is how I would describe it. This situation really helped me to realize that you can't have the best of both worlds until you have paid the full price for success. I couldn't be with my family and go after my dream of playing basketball. Playing at the level I wanted to play and getting the opportunities I wanted would mean I needed to be in America and not at home with my family. This situation also taught me the importance of sacrifice and how hard I had to continue to work so that one day I could both be in America playing basketball and be with my family. On the road to turning your dreams into a reality, what you want won't' be handed to you. You have to go out and get it. You have to work as hard as you can to do what it is that you want to do. I couldn't have the best of both worlds at this time, so I had to sacrifice one or the other and, for now, I sacrificed playing in America.

I told all of my family and friends that I was staying home and they were all excited. Now it was time for me to get in a school. I wanted to go to a school where the majority of my friends were. My dad and I went to a school called C.R. Walker High School and met with the principal. She asked me for my BJC's test scores. The BJC is a national examination that we take in The Bahamas when we are in the ninth grade. I was not able to take it because I left two weeks into the ninth grade. I explained to her that I left when I was thirteen years old and I just needed to get in a school. At first, I thought because I was not able to take the exams, she wouldn't let me in the school, but, by the grace of God, everything worked out. She asked me what kind of kid I was and I told her I would not do anything to get in trouble and she said, "I hope so." I took an English exam and a Math exam and she let me in the school. I was back with all my friends I went to elementary school with and it was super exciting. Although it felt good to be with them, I still wanted to be back in America.

Adjusting

By the time I started school it was January. Basketball tryouts had already come and gone, but I went to the head coach and explained my situation to him. He told me to start coming to practices. I started going to practice and eventually I made the team. We had a pretty solid team that won some games, but we did not win the public school championships. Despite that, I really enjoyed being a part of the team. The school work was very challenging for me at first. I had to study so much more than I did at the school in Florida because the work we did there was not very challenging. I would stay after school to get extra help from my teachers with homework and class work that I could not understand. It was a grind for me. Another reason school was difficult for me was because I did not really want to be there. I wanted to be back in America. I would look on YouTube and see highlight videos of guys I knew from Florida and would think I was falling behind on my game. This was extremely frustrating because I felt like guys were passing me by and getting better than me.

Basketball was not the only sport I participated in at C.R. Walker. I was on the track team as well. I competed in the 100m and 200m and I did pretty well considering the fact that I had not ran track since I was thirteen years old. It was a lot of fun to be back on the track team, but even out there on the field, where I first started, could not compare to the love I now had for the game of basketball. Ironically, sometimes where you start, is not where you will always end up. When I was doing track, I could never see myself doing anything else until I actually tried something different. Most people are afraid to try something different because they feel as if they are only good at one thing, but I have learned in my life that you never know what you are actually good at until you try different things. I continued to study and work hard in school and this caused me to develop a great relationship with me and a few of my teachers. I was also the face of the basketball team and one of the fastest sprinters on the track team, which made me popular at school. The principal liked me, my teachers liked me and my friends were all there, but I still wanted to leave. I had offers to return to America but only from a few schools in Florida but I did not accept them.

There were a few reasons I did not want to return to Florida. The first reason was because I did not want the coach from my old school to see me. I did not want to be around him anymore. The second reason was that I wanted a chance to play ball in the Midwest. I felt like basketball was much bigger out there and I wanted to be a part of that. Being back home also made me realize how bad I wanted to turn my dreams into reality. Think about it: I was home with my family, around all the people I loved and I still wanted to leave. I just knew I would not make the NBA, go to college for free or move my family to America if I stayed home in The Bahamas. There was only one place I could do those things and that was in America. I had mixed emotions about being home. I was happy and grateful I could see my family anytime I wanted to because that wasn't the case when I was in Florida, but I wished I could have seen them anytime I wanted in America.

A couple of months went by and I got word that the school I had been going to in Florida shut down. The school was closed because it was not accredited with the NCAA—meaning that the school standards did not meet the standards of the NCAA. I thanked God so much that I left when I did because it could have been bad; if I hadn't left, I would not have been able to go to Division 1. Following my heart and not worrying about what other people would think paid off for me in this instance. What if I would have stayed in school because of what I thought other people would say or think about me? I would not have been able to be in America anyway because the school shut down. That is why we should not let what other people will think or say about us affect what we decide to do in our lives. I have learned that most of the times when we think people are thinking about us, they really are not. We give people power over us by thinking that they are thinking about what we are doing in our lives when most of the time they aren't even concerned. Don't lose sleep thinking about what someone else might be thinking about you.

Before I moved back home, my mom and dad separated and this time it was for real. So it was back to just me, my dad and my little brother living together. My brother and I saw my mom on the weekends. At sixteen, I was able to handle my parents being separated much better than I was able to when I was growing up. I was older now and seeing them separate so many times helped me deal with it better. I wanted my parents to be together, of course, but I could handle them not being together. My grades weren't dropping in school because of it and I wasn't staying up all night thinking about it. In fact, I was staying up all night thinking about how long it would take me to get back to America. The opportunity was closer than I thought.

One day, my mom called me and told me that a coach from a school in Tallahassee, Florida called her about me. There is a showcase in Freeport, Bahamas that high school and college coaches from America come to and recruit players from. The coach wanted me to participate in it. He had already seen me play before but wanted to meet me in-person and talk about me coming to the school. The school was ranked eighth in the country and, although I did not want to go back to Florida, it was seven hours from Ft. Lauderdale, so I figured it would be a good thing for me. My mom and I got on a plane to go to Freeport. I was extremely excited about this new opportunity. I could not wait to get there to see what would happen. We got off the plane, dropped our stuff off at the hotel and went to the showcase to meet the coach. My mom and I showed up to the gym to find out that the coach was not there. He never showed up. What do you do when someone tells you they are going to be somewhere and they never show up? This was extremely tough to deal with and I reacted how most people would in a situation like that—emotionally. Playing in the showcase wasn't in the plan; I was there to meet the coach but the showcase was taking place regardless. My mom told me I was already there so I needed to play. I played and terribly. The entire time, all I could think about was the coach not showing up. Turnovers, easy shots being missed and making bad plays—I definitely was not playing or feeling like myself.

After the game, I saw a guy talking to my mom. After the way I played, I just knew he couldn't be talking about me. I walked up to him and shook his hand. Instantly I knew that he was the coach I was meant to meet—not the one that was originally supposed to meet at the showcase. We introduced ourselves to each other and he said, "I'm Kyle Lindsted." There were a few more schools that my mom and I talked to at the showcase, but I told my mom that I knew where I needed to go. He told me how much he loved my game and wanted me to be a part of his program. Did he not just see how poorly I played? Quickly, I learned that sometimes people see you for who you are and what you can do even when you don't see it yourself. When I shook Coach Kyle's hand, I knew that wherever he was is where I was supposed to be. Whatever is supposed to happen is going to happen. I wanted to go to that other school with the coach that never showed up, but I was meant to go to Sunrise Christian Academy with Coach Kyle. The coach from the school in Tallahassee never showed up because he wasn't supposed to. It was meant for me to meet Coach Kyle that day because God used him in a special way in my life. Sometimes God doesn't give us what we want. Instead He gives us what we need. A lot of times we don't understand what He is doing, but if we keep the faith, He will reveal it to us.

On the way back home, my mom told me that there was no way she was letting me go to Sunrise without us visiting the school together. She wanted to be there this time to see it for herself. After everything I experienced in Florida, she was not going to let that happen again. Every mother in the world would have done the same thing my mom did had their child experienced what I did. So we went to Sunrise to check it out and it was legit. Everything was as good as could be. After shaking Coach Kyle's hand, I knew that I had to be with him, and after visiting Sunrise, why I should be there made even more sense.

Purpose Principles

1. You can't have the best of both worlds until you have paid the full price for success.

2. Sometimes people will see you for who you are and what you can do even when you don't see it yourself.

3. You never know what you are actually good at until you try something that you have never done before.

4. Don't lose sleep thinking about what someone else thinks about you.

5. Sometimes God doesn't give us what we want. Instead, He gives us what we need.

CHAPTER 12

Tum, Who Are You?

"It only takes one moment for you to realize who you truly are.""

Attending a school in the Midwest was the goal, but when I got the call from the school in Tallahassee, I was ready to make that move; I was going to settle for less than what I actually wanted by going there. Part of my decision to go to the new school was me wanting to get back to America and another part was me actually deciding settling for less than what I wanted. God is so faithful that He will always give us the desires of our hearts. Playing at a showcase for a school in Florida ultimately led to me going to a school in Kansas, which is in the Midwest. I was upset that the coach from Tallahassee never showed up, but God reminded me that I never wanted to go there in the first place. A school in the Midwest is what I desired and that is what He gave me. Through that process, God showed me that settling for less is never an option and that if I keep trusting in Him, He will give me the desires of my heart.

I left home again for Sunrise Christian Academy in Kansas. I was excited to start this new journey in my life and super thankful for the opportunity. When I first got there, something happened that really opened up my eyes. I was talking to this guy, Jared Pitchman, at the gym one day about what it means to be saved. I told him that if you are saved and you sin, you have to go up to the altar each time and recommit your life to God. He told me that I did not have to do that every time.

He said to me, "Tum, once you get saved, God has you in the palm of His hand forever. You don't have to go to the altar every single time you sin to recommit your life to Him."

I continued to tell him that we had to go up to the altar every single time we sinned and I was pretty confident in that. He was also confident in what he was saying. To help his argument, he called his dad, Ron, and his dad explained to me the same exact thing Jared did. That once I got saved, I did not have to continually go up to the altar every time I went to church. That was exactly what I was doing. I was in complete shock because, although I did not agree with what Jared was saying, after his dad explained the same thing to me, it made a lot of sense. Jesus died on the cross for every sin we would ever commit knowingly and unknowingly. Because of this, we wouldn't have to recommit our lives to him every time we sinned. That was extremely powerful to me. I don't like to use the word "religion" or "religious," but I never grew up in a religious home. My parents and I did not go to church every Sunday. I never grew up praying with my mom and dad, but religion was something that all public schools back home taught. It was a class in school; it was a part of the curriculum. The only times my family and I went to church was for an occasion like Christmas, New Year's Eve or a funeral. Church was not a significant part of my life, but I always knew there was a God. When I was in Florida, I started reading the Bible by myself, but I couldn't understand it very well. Being at Sunrise helped me with that tremendously. We would go to church every Sunday. We had Chapel every Wednesday in school and we had Bible study with Dr. Lindsted who is Coach Kyle's dad. Dr. Lindsted broke down the Bible in ways I had never heard before. He played a huge role in me understanding God's word. I could listen to him talk about scriptures for hours.

At Sunrise, the living situation and the school were so much better than the school before. The first house I lived in was a four-bedroom house with three bathrooms for everyone to use. We had an actual school, challenging school work and our own practice gym that was available to us 24/7. This was what I was expecting the first time I left home, but maybe if I would have gotten all of the things I expected, I would not have appreciated it the way I did at Sunrise. Maybe not having all those things at first prepared me so that I could appreciate it more when I did get it. Sometimes in life, not having what you want when you want it makes you appreciate getting what you want when it is time for you to have it. Basketball practices were so much better because they weren't outside in the sun, but they were very challenging at the same time. We would run a lot but nothing like I did at the other school. The running at the other school felt like punishment but at Sunrise it felt like we were conditioning to get ourselves in shape.

Some days in practice, I would encourage my teammates and other days I wouldn't. Some days in the weight room I would encourage my teammates and other days I stayed to myself and didn't say a word to anyone. Whenever I did encourage and motivate my teammates, it would really inspire them. But like I said, this was not something I did every day. I honestly did not care enough or think anything of doing it every day. I encouraged my teammates when I felt like it. Then I would be cool and casual on the court and pretend to be a player that I wasn't. One of the biggest reasons I was staying to myself and not motivating and inspiring people every day was because of everything I went through at the other school. I honestly did not know who I was. I was letting what I experienced in the past determine who I was in the present. A lot of people are currently struggling with the same issue. One day I would be full of energy and the next day I appeared to have none at all. There was no consistency in who I was, but that would change quickly.

I had no idea that every day Coach Kyle was watching how I was acting. One day, I came to the weight room and I did not say anything to anyone. Then I went to practice and I did the same exact thing and, on top of that, I was cool and casual. I remember this like it was yesterday: Coach Kyle pulled me to the side after practice, looked me dead in my eyes and said, "You will never be Kobe Bryant and you will never be LeBron James."

As he is saying this to me, I'm looking at him and wondering what he was talking about, but I knew he was speaking the truth. Still, it caught me off guard and at first I did not like it. Most people say they want the truth, but if it's not packaged the way they want it, all of a sudden they no longer want it.

"You will never be Kobe Bryant or LeBron James, but you have a gift. I have never seen someone motivate and inspire another person like you do. Be who you are, Tum. That is who you are. You are a born leader and you motivate and inspire like I have never seen before."

After that day I never reverted back to trying to be something I wasn't. I inspired my teammates every single day after that. It only takes one moment for you to realize who you truly are and that was my moment. That moment when Coach Kyle was not afraid to tell me what I needed to hear instead of what I wanted to hear changed my life. We need people in our lives who will tell us what we need to hear because what we need to hear is way more important than what we want to hear. Coach Kyle wasn't the only one who told me what I needed to hear. At the end of my sophomore year, I met a guy named Matt Suther. He is the founder of the AAU organization, Mokan Elite, a summer basketball league. That is the AAU team I played for. Matt never sugar-coated anything he said. He is what you would call a straight shooter. If someone needs to be held accountable, he is going to do it. That's the way he is. One day, we had two practices and he wasn't at the first one. In the first practice, I rolled my ankle twice. The second time I rolled my ankle, I hit the floor with my hand and yelled extremely loud. Honestly, I was acting like a little baby. Matt heard about it and waited until after the second practice to approach me. He said, "Man, what's going on with you? Why are you acting like that? Yelling like something is wrong. Don't get comfortable because you got offers rolling in. You never do that. Don't change who you are. Don't let that happen again." The entire time he was looking me in the eye and I was looking him in his. At the time, I was saying to myself, "Man, what are you talking about? I'm not changing." Matt got on me because even though I hadn't change, he wanted to make sure I didn't, so he called me out. In other words, I shouldn't have acted out like I did and

Matt was not going to let me think it was okay for me to do that, especially when I had never done it before. I was just caught up in the moment. Did it hurt rolling my ankle twice? Of course it did. But we are going to get hurt a lot in life and other people are watching how we respond. Matt did not like the way I responded to that situation and he told me what I needed to hear. That is how it was playing for Mokan. They get you ready for life. They aren't afraid to tell you what you need to hear. That's what made playing for that program so special. They helped me become not only a better player but, more importantly, a better man. Matt and his wife, Cherie, both hold a special place in my heart. They welcomed me to the program with open arms and became my family and will be for life.

We had a pretty good team at Sunrise, but there was a guy on our team by the name of Buddy Hield who was being recruited by a lot of Division 1 schools. We would play open gym and they would all come to see him, so the gym would be filled with high-level and well-known college coaches from all over the country. One day, we were playing open gym and all the schools that had offered him scholarships were in attendance. I played extremely well that day and ended up receiving my first college offer from the University of Oklahoma. This was a proud day in my life because this was one of the reasons I left home at such a young age. Receiving my first opportunity to play college basketball for free meant the world to me. Oklahoma called Coach Kyle to give him the news and then he told me. This motivated me to work so much harder because I wanted more offers. Not only did I want more offers, but I wanted to get better at the game. One day, our strength and conditioning coach, Bret Michael, came over to the house. I was sitting in my room and he came in and asked me, "Tum, how great do you want to be?" I said, "I want to be really great!" Then he said, "If you want to be great, you have to do something that other high school players aren't doing." I asked, "And what is that?" He said, "Meet me in the gym at 4:30 am." The next day, I met him in the gym at that time and it became a routine. The time would fluctuate between 4:30 am and 5:30 am but we always met. Coach Bret pushed me extremely hard and I accomplished more by 7:30 am than the average high school player had done in their entire day. I was committed to getting better and Coach was committed to helping me get better. All of my other coaches were also committed to helping me get better as well: Coach Jeremiah, Coach Luke and Coach Joey. They each woke up early in the morning on different days to push me too.

Buddy, and I lived in the same house and after practice one day we talked. He said, "Bro, tell me about you." I asked, "What do you want to know?" He said, "Every time I look to my right or my left during a sprint, you are there. Every time I go to the gym, you are there. Why are you like that?" I then explained to him everything I had gone through up to that point in my life.

He then said, "Now I see why you work so hard." After I told Buddy my story, he pushed me hard every day; he understood and respected my drive. We both were so competitive that there were times Coach Kyle banned us from playing open gym because it would turn into a one-on-one battle. We never were on the same team in practice and we used to play one-on-one for hours. Many of those games almost ended in fights, but there were no hard feelings. We just wanted to make each other better. Off the floor, we were the best of friends. Put yourself around people who are going to push you to be the best you can be. That is very important on the road to success. We were and still are super close to this day. We made sure we pushed each other no matter what. That's what real friends do. They push each other.

Throughout my high school career at Sunrise, I continued to get better at the game. Because of that, I became well-known around the country and had offers from many different schools. This would prove itself by me being invited to some high level camps as a junior in high school. I got invited to the LeBron James Skills Academy, the Kyrie Irving and Deron Williams Point Guard Camp and the Nike Global Challenge. All of these camps were by invitation only and I was the first one in the history of my school to attend any of those. Hard work was paying off and I was experiencing things I had never expected to do but that were the perks of all of my hard work. My senior year of high school I was a McDonald's All-American nominee; to be nominated for such a game and not even be American was very un-usual, an honor and something I will always remember. It did not matter where I was from, what really mattered was where I was going and the skills I had gotten, from all of my hard work, that would get me there. A lot of times in life people don't go where they want to because they get caught up in thinking about where they are from. All that really matters is how hard you are willing to work to get where you are trying to go.

My sophomore year we finished with a 19-4 record and my junior year we finished with a 29-1 record. It was time for my senior year. The offers were still pouring in from many schools, but it was now time to cut my list down. My offers from schools included Indiana, Oklahoma, Kansas, Kansas State, Iowa, Creighton, Ole Miss, Memphis, Minnesota and SMU. There were other schools as well and I also had high interest from many schools, which meant that I was very close to getting an offer from them. At the beginning of August in my se-nior year, I cut my list down to Indiana, Minnesota, and Oklahoma. This was a very difficult process for me be-cause I had to call all the other schools and thank them for recruiting me. I had built great relationships with some of the coaches, but I had to do what I thought was best for me and those were the three schools that I decided to take official visits to.

Purpose Principles

1. Never settle for less just because you feel like you need to rush to get to where you want to go.

2. Sometimes in life not having what you want when you want it makes you appreciate getting what you want more when it is time for you to have it.

3. Don't let what you experienced in the past determine who you become in the future.

4. It only takes one moment for you to realize who you truly are.

5. Having people in your life who tell you what you need to hear instead of what you want to hear is very critical on the road to success.

CHAPTER 13

I Set This Up Just For You

My first official visit was at Minnesota and it went really well. My next visit was to Oklahoma and it was great because they were the first school to offer me a scholarship, and on top of that, Buddy was there. I thought I only had one visit left to take and that was at Indiana, but that wasn't the case. One day, I was doing homework after school and before practice in one of the classrooms. I had to take ten classes my senior year of high school in order to make up for the classes that I had taken at the school in Florida that didn't count since the school wasn't accredited. Among the classes I had to retake in senior year was freshman English while taking senior English too. I had no lunch breaks my senior year of high school, but one of my teachers, Mrs. Gerber, allowed me to eat lunch during the time I had her class. One day, Coach Kyle walked in the classroom and asked me, "Tum, if Kentucky, Michigan State, or UCLA want to jump back in on your recruitment, would you let them?"

I said to him, "It depends on which one it is."

They were all schools that had interest in me but never gave me an offer. I was hoping the offer would be from Kentucky because that was my dream school. My heart was beating extremely fast because I had no idea who he was going to say. We walked down to his office and he told me Dane Fife from Michigan State called for me.

"Coach, let them in," I told him.

I had no idea why I said it so quickly, but I did. I talked to Coach Fife that day and later that night I talked to Coach Tom Izzo. The entire time we were on the phone, it felt like we had known each other for a while. We talked as if we had met before. After I let them in on my recruitment, Coach Kyle made me call the other three schools to let them know that I would be taking a visit to Michigan State. I did not want to make the calls. I asked Coach Kyle if he would call for me but he wouldn't. He told me that it was a part of being a man and it was something that I had to do myself. The other three coaches received my call and they weren't happy about it. Coach Crean from Indiana told me to make sure that Indiana was my last visit and they were. The next day, I was on a flight to East Lansing. Before getting on the flight, I had to call my mom and let her know that she would be coming to East Lansing so we could visit Michigan State together. It caught her completely off guard because she knew that they hadn't been on my list. I got to Michigan State on a Thursday and my mom arrived that Friday. I had no idea what to expect on this visit, but I learned that some of the best things in life happen when you least expect them to. I had already visited Oklahoma and Minnesota and both schools had enough time to prepare for my arrival. I decided to visit Michigan State one day before going so I wasn't sure how it would go because they had no time to prepare for me. I literally had to leave school in the middle of the day, go home and pack a bag so I could head to the airport.

When I got to Michigan State it felt like I was back at Sunrise. At Sunrise, we were all about family and on my visit to MSU, I felt like they were the same. Throughout my recruiting process, one thing I always thought about was how my parents and other family members would not be able to see me play live, so I wanted to be a part of a program that would be my family away from my family. Many people asked me how I would know the right place for me. "I'm just going to follow my heart," was always my answer. "I will just know what school is the right one for me." I knew that school would feel like home and my teammates would feel like family.

My hosts were Travis Trice and Matt Costello and they were both amazing people. Although they were my hosts, I spent time with all of the other players as well. Something that really stood out to me on my visit took place when we went to the football game. As we were walking on the football field, Adreian Payne, another one of the basketball players, put his arms around me and for some reason that just made me feel at home. I could tell it was genuine. It wasn't phony and nothing like that had happened at my visit to the other two schools. I'm not saying the other two visits were phony; I just hadn't experienced anything like that. That was an eye-opener for me.

I enjoyed the football game and even met some of the Spartan legends like Mateen Cleaves and Travis Walton. They were amazing people and I could remember Travis and I talking almost the entire time I was at the football game. We shared the same passion for basketball and we also talked about where we were from and things we wanted to accomplish in life. It felt as if I knew him my entire life. After the football game, we walked over to the offices and it was time for me, my mom, Coach Kyle and Coach Izzo to meet. I listened to them talk for most of the time but then Coach Izzo said he had heard that I was a kid who appreciated everything I had. I remembered him saying that me coming there would be, "a match made in Heaven." That was the kind of per-son he was looking for—someone who would fit into their culture and system. He asked me what Coach Kyle meant to me and I told him that, "I would die for him because he changed my life." Coach Kyle had six kids yet he treated me like I was one of his and was always honest with me. We are extremely close and he be-lieved in me sometimes more than I believed in myself.

They continued to talk and out of nowhere I heard a voice saying, "Tum, Tum, I set this up just for you." That was one of the first times in my life that I heard God speak loud and clear. It was something I could not ignore and it was then in that meeting I knew I was going to be a Spartan. I didn't say anything to my mom or Coach Kyle right away. However, when we got back to Wichita, I told Coach Kyle that I was going to MSU. I told him that there was nothing I could see at Indiana that would make me change my mind. Honestly, I didn't even want to take my Indiana visit after my MSU one because I knew that there would be nothing that I would experience there that would change my mind. Coach Kyle made me go on to Indiana visit because he said it wouldn't be professional if I didn't. I knew though that nothing would be able to change my mind about going to MSU because I was sure that I heard God tell me that He set it up just for me. He doesn't make mistakes, so there was no way I wasn't going to go to MSU. Kentucky could have called and offered me a scholarship and I still wouldn't have changed my mind. I was going to go to MSU.

I took my visit to Indiana the following week and my body was there but my mind wasn't. All I could think about was what I heard from God in the meeting that day at MSU. The Indiana visit was great, but my heart was already set. When I got back from my Indiana visit, there was about a week that I did not take any phone calls from the coaches on my list. I used that time to appreciate everything that had happened in my life thus far and also tell people who were close to me where I was going to be playing college basketball. On September 26, 2013, starting around 8:30 am, I called all the schools that were on my list. I called Minnesota, Indiana and Oklahoma and thanked all the head coaches for recruiting me. Being a kid from The Bahamas, it was special to me to have options of where I wanted to play college basketball. I told them I did not take that for granted when they recruited me. After calling those three schools, my last call was to MSU. I called Coach Izzo and as the phone rang I couldn't believe that I was about to commit. He answered the phone and said, "Hello, Tum. How you doing buddy?"

I said, "Coach, you ready to win another national championship?" He just shouted with excitement and said, "Are you serious?!!!"

That is how I committed to MSU: I told Coach Izzo and then around 10 am, I had an announcement ceremony at my high school. All my friends and teammates were there. The only ones who weren't there were my family members back home in Nassau. After I committed to MSU, the gym went crazy. Everyone was so happy for me. It was one of the best days of my life—to see a part of my dream come true, which was to be able to play college basketball for free. It was extremely humbling. My phone was blowing up and my name was blowing up on all social media platforms. After I announced where I was going to school, President Obama's and my name were trending on Twitter. So many people sent me text messages; I got text messages from all the players on the MSU team and they were all saying how excited they were to have as me a part of the family now. I was still in shock from seeing my name trending with President Obama's. Then all of a sudden I got a text message from Draymond Green. He also congratulated me and told me welcome to the family. That entire day was exciting for me. When I lay down that night, I cried because it felt so great to be able to see a part of my dream come true. I thanked God so much for making all of it happen for me. Everything that happened made me even more motivated; I knew that I had to keep going because there was more work to be done. My senior year went by pretty fast and was emotional for me because Sunrise changed my life. Coach Kyle made me believe in who I was and I was super grateful for that. It was hard for me to leave, but it was a chapter in my life that had to be closed. Now I was on my way to MSU to walk into what I was told by God was set up JUST for me. I thought He was only talking about basketball but He also had other things in mind.

Purpose Principles

1. Some of the best things in life happen when you least expect them to.

2. You will know the right thing for you if you just follow your heart.

3. Having someone in your life who believes in you more than you believe in yourself sometimes, is a key to your success.

4. Don't take for granted any opportunities you get in life.

5. On the road to success, achievements shouldn't satisfy you, they should motivate you.

CHAPTER 14

Freshman Season

Wichita to East Lansing was a very long drive. However, I wasn't the one driving, Coach Kyle was. On my way to campus, I got a text message from Draymond asking when I was getting to campus and I told him I would be there soon. Pulling up to the dorms, I thought to myself, "Wow, this is my new home." I was very excited about it and couldn't wait to get started on the next chapter in my life. When it was time for our first weight room workout, I wasn't allowed to participate until I took a physical. I remember just standing in the weight room, watching the guys and one of my teammates, Denzel Valentine, said, "Come over here. You're a part of the team."

The first summer Draymond was on campus with us and he worked out with us every single day. It was great to be around him and learn from him because we all were trying to go where he was—the NBA. Just like at Sunrise, I encouraged, motivated and inspired all of my teammates as soon as I got to MSU. The only difference was when I first got to Sunrise I did it sometimes because I did not know who I was, but at MSU, I did it all the time because I now knew who I was and wasn't going to change. My energy and the way I was able to motivate and inspire were at an all-time high. We had a lot of great players on the team so I figured the only way I would play was to do something that no one else could do on a consistent basis. It did not matter what we were doing, I wanted to make sure I was always encouraging, motivating and pushing my teammates—trying to bring the best out of them because they were doing the same for me. I was doing it at a level like never before; my ability to motivate was so high that Draymond noticed and it moved him to go in Coach Izzo's office and tell him that he should make me the team captain. A compliment like that coming from a player and person like Draymond blew my mind completely because I had no idea that he thought that highly of me. I still think about that often.

One of the things I worried about the most going into college was if I would find real friends—people who would care about me for who I am and not what I do. One day, I grabbed Marvin Clark, Jr. and Javon Bess, my two roommates, and knocked on every door in the dorms, introducing ourselves. I don't know what moved me to want to do that, but I did. We ended up meeting four girls: Sydney, Ashleigh, Jessica and Janay. They would become my really close friends, apart from my teammates. I still wonder if we had never knocked on every door, would I have met them? They are my little sisters and they all hold a special place in my heart.

I was happy that I had made friends at school but they didn't replace my family who I missed so much every day. Being away from my family and especially my mom was hard my freshman year. I was used to having my mom at all my games when I was a kid. Now that I had made it to Division 1, I wanted her to watch me play now more than ever. It was in that year that I met Amy and Kevin Miller. Mr. Miller, who I called K-Mill, knew Coach Izzo and would come and watch our team practice sometimes. K-Mill would invite the team to his son, Drew's, birthday party ever year—even before I came to MSU. My freshman year, my team went to Drew's birthday party as they always did and that's how I developed a friendship with The Millers. Mrs. Miller, who I called A-Mill, and I exchanged telephone numbers. She and I talked from time-to-time. Over my four years of college, she became my second mom, The Millers became my second family, their kids, Cole, Madi and Drew became my brothers and sisters and their house became my home away from home. The Millers did so much for me and will always hold a special place in my heart.

My first year, practice started and I was pretty much prepared for how hard it would be since we practiced hard at Sunrise. They were harder than my high school practices but my high school team and my AAU team, Mokan, did an unbelievable job of preparing me. We even did some of the same drills at MSU that we did in high school. However, the players at MSU were so much better than the ones at Sunrise and the game was now much faster. I was running around like a chicken with my head cut off for the first two months. As I watched film and talked to the coaches, everything slowed down for me. The game at the collegiate level started to make more sense to me. We started playing games and we were doing okay. There were a bunch of close games at first and we could not close those games out. At the beginning of the season, I was coming off the bench playing behind senior point guard, Travis Trice. He was my roommate when we were on the road and he took me under his wing. Whenever I did not understand something in practice, he was always the one to pull me to the side and help me out with it. I was so blessed that he was there.

We were losing some games we should have won but turnovers hurt us a lot and most of the games we were losing were by two points. I remember us losing a game to Texas Southern University and that was a very bad loss for us. That was a team that had no business beating us, but they did because we did not do what we were supposed to do to win. We were winning some games and losing some, trying to figure out who we were as a team. Now it was time to go into Big Ten Play. Our first game was on the road at Iowa. I was still coming off the bench. When it was time for me to check in the game, Iowa was going on a run. I sat down by the scorer's table and I had never heard a gym that loud before. I don't know if I was so nervous that it made the gym sound louder than it actually was or if it was just that loud. I checked in to the game and actually ended up playing pretty well. Trice and I played a lot together in the second half. We won that game. That was a huge win for us going into our home opener.

We started to play better, but we still lost a couple games we shouldn't have. I was still coming off the bench and had not started in a game yet. We started to adjust our starting lineup and I got my first start at home in January when we played Indiana. That was one of my best games thus far and we won by 20. It meant so much to me to be able to start, especially because I had come all the way from The Bahamas for this opportunity. Also, playing for a great coach in one of the best programs in the country, I wanted to not only play my best but to win. Starting was special to me. We won that game but Trice was back in the starting lineup the next game because we were changing lineups, trying to see what would be best for our team. I was a defender, an energy guy, who ran the team when I was out there and Trice was a complete scorer. He could score at all three levels. We had very different games and our games fit perfectly together. More games went by and we lost another game we should have won. It was at home to Illinois. We went in to practice the day after we lost to Illinois and I was told that I was going to be the starting point guard.

We won our next four games and Trice came off the bench. We both played a lot of minutes together. It wasn't that I was a better player than Trice, but me starting and him coming off the bench was better for our team because we brought different things to the team. Like I said earlier, Trice was my roommate and when I first became the starting point guard, I thought this would hurt our relationship, but it didn't at all. He was still helping me out in practice every day, making sure I was doing the right things. I appreciated that so much because I felt as if that would not have been the case at any other school. People may have looked at it like I was taking his position, but I wasn't. It was just best for our team that I start and he come off the bench. He was putting up big numbers and was playing his best basketball of the season coming off the bench. Before we knew it, we were both in the starting lineup. The team was much better and we were winning games people thought we should lose.

We finished the Big Ten season with a record of 12-6 and now it was time for the Big Ten Tournament. We made it all the way to the championship game. We played Ohio State in the first game, Maryland in the second and lost to Wisconsin in the championship game after being up most of the game. That was a tough loss to deal with, but we knew we could not worry about that too much because it was time for us to make a run in the NCAA Tournament. Before the season started, I had seen an article that said our team wasn't supposed to be very good and that it would be a rebuilding year for the program. But it didn't matter what people said because our eyes were on making it to Indianapolis, which was where the Final Four would be played. Before our loss to Texas Southern, we would break every huddle saying, "Indy on three." After our loss to Texas Southern, instead of saying Indy on three, we said, "Beat [the name of the team we were playing in that particular game]." We focused on the current team, but Indy was still on our minds.

Final Four Run

The first game of the NCAA tournament, we played Georgia and won that game. The second game we played against a tough Virginia team and ended up winning that game as well. Now we are on our way to the Sweet 16 and this was going to be a tough match-up. This was a big game for me personally because I was playing against one of my closest friends and former high school teammates, Buddy Hield, from the University of Oklahoma. Everyone back home was tuned into that game and we beat Oklahoma as well. Now we were one game away from going to a Final Four. No one, besides us, thought that we could make it that far. Sometimes in life only you have to believe in what it is that you want to achieve. You believing that you can do what most people think you can't is enough for you to do it. We were only one game away from Indy and it had been a tough road, but this game would be the toughest. We played against Louisville and ended up beating them in overtime. When the buzzer went off, I ran to the middle of the court and hugged my teammate, Marvin Clark, Jr., and we both said, "We did it!" Marvin became one of my closest friends while playing for the same AAU team, Mokan. We then went on to play high school basketball together at Sunrise and both ended up playing at Michigan State. Making the Final Four was something we always talked about doing. That was one of the best moments of our lives. With tears of joy running down my face, thinking about everything that I had been through in my life, it was a surreal moment. We got up on stage and were still on live TV when my mom called one of my coach's phone. I grabbed the phone and said, "Momma, we going to the Final Four!" Words can't explain what that felt like. We were finally on our way to Indy.

In Indianapolis, we would match up against one of the best teams in the country, Duke. This was a revenge game for us because they had beaten us at the beginning of the season. The day before the game, both teams had an open practice and I remember looking around saying to myself, "Wow! Only God can do this." I could barely sleep that night because I was so excited to play in the game.

It was game day and I sat down and thought about all the ups and downs our team went through the entire year. We were at this point because no matter what came our way, we stuck together and we made it work.

All the practices, all the late nights and early mornings were worth it. On the bus, on the way to the game, all I could think about was leaving home at thirteen years old. I also thought about how every little kid back home will be watching the game and will be inspired to believe that they can achieve the same thing; they can do anything they want to do in life. I was an example for them and that was an amazing feeling. We got to the arena and did our normal pre-game routines. Then it was time to play the game. They called my name for the starting lineups and here I was, a kid from Nassau, Bahamas, starting in a Final Four as a freshman. I was only one of just three freshmen to start as point guard under Coach Izzo and only the second one to start in a Final Four. How could I come from sleeping in a one-bedroom with rats crawling over me some nights and bathing in a tin tub outside to starting in a Final Four, playing in front of 70,000 people and think it had anything to do with me making it happen? It was God who had made all of this happen. There was no possible way for me to be able to make it to that point without Him giving me the strength to do so every day. We ended up losing that game by 20 points and as a competitor that hurt really bad. But at the end of the day, there was no reason for us to hang our heads because we did something that many people didn't think we were capable of. That is what happens in life when you believe in yourself and keep going no matter what you face—you end up doing things only you believe you can do.

Purpose Principles

1. Bringing the best out of someone else eventually brings the best out of you.

2. When you don't do the things you are supposed to do to win, you will lose.

3. When your eyes are set on your dreams, it won't matter to you what other people say about you.

4. You believing that you can do what most people think you can't is enough for you to do it.

5. When you believe in yourself and keep going no matter what you face, you end up doing things only you believe you can do.

CHAPTER 15

Dreams Do Come True

My career at MSU was completely the opposite of what I thought it would be, especially on the court. Remember earlier when I said I heard God say to me, "I set this up just for you" and I thought it was only about basketball? I would learn throughout my career that it had nothing to do with basketball; I really thought it was about basketball because we made it to the Final Four my freshman year and I was the starting point guard. But I was wrong. My senior year of high school, I built a relationship with Eric Thomas, better known as ET, The Hip Hop Preacher. He's recognized as the number one motivational speaker in the world. When I got to MSU, we first met at about 5 am one morning and I thought that was pretty cool, but I had no idea what our relationship would do for my life.

Most people did not think our team would ever get to the Final Four. The next year when I was a sophomore, we were even better as a team and had hopes of getting back to the Final Four and also winning the national championship. There was no doubt in our minds that we would do it because we had a better team and were getting off to the best start in program history. We got to the Final Four the first year so we thought that we would definitely get there the second year. But again I was wrong. We won a Big Ten Tournament Championship, got a number two seed in the NCAA tournament and lost in the first game to a fifteenth seed. I learned so much that year; one of the biggest lessons I learned was how to lead and play while being injured. The entire year I played with plantar fasciitis and was in a walking boot for seven months. I would practice and play but had to put the boot on right after the practices and the games. This was difficult to deal with, but I had to go through it. Just because you did something once before doesn't mean that you are automatically going to do it again. My team and I were better than the year before, but that didn't matter because we didn't make the Final Four. I didn't let myself stay focused on the loss that season. You can't focus on past success while on your journey. Focusing on what you did in the past can cause you to lose sight of what you can do and have to do in the present.

I started working for Eric Thomas during the summers. This led to me speaking and sharing my story in high schools around Michigan. I began to develop a passion for speaking because it came so natural to me. While working with him, God told me why He sent me to this earth. He sent me here to motivate, inspire and serve. I had no idea that having a relationship with ET would help me to find my purpose in life. We would talk all the time, pray every morning and meet whenever we could. We have a divine relationship that was set up by God before the foundation of the world. ET is a huge part of why I am who I am today; what God has set up just for me had nothing to do with basketball.

My Junior Year

Going into my junior year, two of my best friends, Marvin Clark, Jr. and Javon Bess, transferred from MSU. This was very hard for me to deal with because we were super close—so close that we all have matching tattoos on the left side of our legs that says, "3Each." We came up with the idea for the tattoo as a twist on the saying, "To each his own." Marvin, Javon and I did everything together. Even though they left school that year, we remain super close to this day. It's crazy to me how a game could connect me to people that I will have relationships with for life. That's what we have—a bond and connection that will last forever.

I missed my friends all throughout that year but I continued working with ET and speaking in schools when one day I heard God say to me, "Start a Bible study." "No way," I replied.

I thought that there was no way He wants me to start a Bible study. I wasn't doing it. We had a great class coming in my junior year with Miles Bridges, Joshua Langford, Nick Ward and Cassius Winston on the team. It was in our DNA as a team to always want to push and make a run for another Final Four. With this class coming in, that's what we wanted to do again. Miles, Joshua, Nick and Cassius all became my little brothers, but there was a special bond between Josh, Miles and me. I can't really explain the bond we had, but I know that it was divine. When something is divine it makes up for time—meaning that I felt like I had known them way longer than I actually had. They would stay at my apartment all the time and we would talk for hours. I know for sure that God placed the both of them in my life for a reason. Like I said earlier, Marvin, Javon and I were and still are really close. Then I was sitting down one day and something came to me: When Marvin and Javon left, Miles and Josh came. I then looked at this correlation between all of them; Miles and Marvin, Joshua and Javon. Marvin is light-skinned and Miles is light-skinned. Joshua is dark-skinned and Javon is dark-skinned. Miles is left-handed, Marvin is left-handed, Joshua is right-handed and Javon is right-handed. Crazy, right? I know. Just like Marvin, Javon and I did everything together; it was the same for Josh, Miles and me—we also did everything together. These were relationships that were bigger than the game of basketball. I would lay down my life for those guys and I know they would do the same for me. It wasn't until Miles and Josh came to MSU that I started the Bible study group. I tell Josh all the time that he plays a major role in me being who I am today. It wasn't until after I knew he was coming to Michigan State that I really started getting my spiritual life right. I knew that Josh was a very spiritual guy, so I wanted to make sure I could help him in any way I could. It's funny how the people we think we are going to help in life, end up helping us instead. My life would be different today had God not placed Miles and Josh in my life. I could tell you a million stories about things we've been through and encountered together. Maybe I will save those for my next book. The first night of Bible study, there were about four people in total that came to it, but I didn't mind because I never ever saw myself having a Bible study in the first place.

My junior season had begun and we were having Bible study when our schedules allowed it. More and more people started to show up and began to talk about how the Bible study was changing their lives. We barely made the NCAA Tournament and we only won 20 games. We lost in the second round of the tournament; that year was very challenging. Leading a team with so many freshmen was tough and there was pressure on us to keep the NCAA Tournament winning streak alive. Keep in mind that all throughout my first three years of college I hadn't had a season where I averaged five or more points. I was a McDonald's All-American nominee coming out of high school and I was doing basically nothing on the court. At least nothing that I had imagined I would do coming out of high school. In my mind, on the court I was underachieving, but in the things that really mattered, I was doing what I never even dreamt of. I was facilitating Bible studies, speaking to high schools and detention centers; through speaking and sharing my story, I was inspiring people to want to be better and touching the lives of so many people. Doing what I felt was so little on the court during my first three years at times made me question if I still wanted to play the game. Coming out of high school, my goal was to be in college for about three years then leave for the NBA. I believed I would be good enough to do that after three years. However, with the way things were going on the court, there was no way that could happen. Teams weren't guarding me, so it was like playing four-on-five when I was out there. I would work on my jumper all the time, but I was afraid to miss in the games, so I didn't shoot. Everyone was saying I couldn't shoot the ball, but I was actually not a bad shooter. I just had no confidence in my ability to shoot, so I started to believe what other people were saying about me. I learned the hard way that when you believe what other people say about you, you will become whatever they call you . . . but only if you continue to believe what they say.

With basketball, nothing was going the way I thought it would go. In terms of the impact I was having on so many lives, I never dreamed of being able to inspire people in the way that God was allowing me to. By the end of my third year, I had won the most inspirational player award for the third straight year at our basketball banquet. It was then that I realized that basketball was not my life anymore. Basketball had meant so much to me that I moved away from my family at a very young age to play the game. I never thought I could love anything more than playing basketball, but I found something I loved more—that was motivating, inspiring and serving people. I was now holding Bible studies, teaching the word of God and leading the team the best way I could.

My Senior Year

My senior year, the Bible study group continued to grow. The numbers went from four to twelve, then to fifteen, then in the twenties. People just kept coming because God was moving in their lives. Our freshmen players from last year had a year full of experience. They were all of our best players on the team and we were the favorites to win the national championship. That did not go according to our plans. My senior year ended up being the toughest year of them all. We had to deal with so many things that we had no control over and it was hard to stay focused. Coach always told us that if we could limit distractions, it would help us, but I felt there were just too many distractions. Despite it all, we stuck together and got through it.

We won the Big Ten outright championship on my senior night, which was very special. We went on to the NCAA Tournament and lost in the second round to Syracuse. We were the favorites to win it all and we came up short. We did not do what everyone expected us to do. More importantly, we didn't do what we expected ourselves to do. Sometimes in life people are going to have high expectations for you. The pressure of what others expect of you never bothers you when you have higher expectations for yourself. Although we did not achieve our goal of winning the national champion- ship, it didn't mean that we were failures. Just because you don't achieve a specific goal doesn't mean that you failed. It just means you missed that mark. When you don't do what you set out to do, keep trying until you get the job done. If you don't pass an exam, don't just drop out of school. Instead, study harder. If you do not reach your goals, don't just quit. Work harder. Unfor- tunately for me, that was my last chance of winning a national championship as a player. I realized it was not about me winning another championship; it was really about the people that I was able to have an impact on. My not winning a national championship didn't define who I was or am. I was blessed to be able to do many great things and go to many great places at Michigan State. I learned a lot about myself. But one of the most valuable things I learned was from Coach Izzo. He taught me how to lead my best friends. He used to tell me, "Good leaders can lead anyone, but great leaders can lead their best friends." What he meant was that I shouldn't be afraid to push the people who are closest to me. I should be able to tell them when they're not doing their jobs. Holding your best friends account- able isn't as easy as it sounds. But like Coach Izzo used to say to me, "If you really love that person and he or she is really your friend, wouldn't you hold them accountable?" That stuck out to me because that goes for every area of life. All the other coaches: Coach Garland, Coach DJ and Coach Fife, taught me valuable lessons as well and played a major part in who I am today. I could talk to Coach Garland about anything for hours. Coach DJ always gave me confidence and knows the game of basketball at an unbelievable level and Coach Fife made that call four years ago to Coach Kyle. I thank Coach Fife all the time for making that call. Had he not called, I might have never been at Michigan State, but God knew what He was doing the whole time.

Graduation Day

May 4, 2018, I did something I never dreamed of as a kid. I walked across a stage in the Breslin Center and graduated with a degree in Communication. Walking across that stage was the result of what happens when you never give up on your dreams. When you don't give up and you keep going, you accomplish not only your dream but also things that you never dreamed of doing. When I was growing up in The Bahamas, my friends and I never talked about going to college; we talked about making it out the hood. Graduating from college was never on our minds. I remember hugging my mom after graduation and her crying so hard that I could feel her tears. For some reason, I got an image in my head of her in the doctor's office as a teenager when the doctor told her she would never be able to have kids. Now, she had just watched her son walk across a stage with a degree—something she could probably never have seen happening. The beautiful thing was that I never gave up. I became the first in my family to graduate from college. My mom didn't go to college and my dad dropped out of high school. I started a new legacy in my family and because I did, my little brother will be graduating college next year. There is something that you will start in your family if you keep going. People are watching you.

One night at Bible study during my senior year, I had up to sixty people sitting in my living room to hear God's word. I could not imagine or ever dream of that happening, but God saw it before the foundation of the world. People's lives were changed because I never gave up. Everything I ever went through in my life I now know had nothing to do with me; it had everything to do with the people I was born to reach. There are going to be things that happen in your life that you will not be able to understand. In life, there are going to be days you feel like you can't take anymore but keep going. There is a saying that goes, "Giving up is never an option." I don't believe that to be true. Giving up is always an option, it is just an option that you should NEVER choose. There are so many people counting on you. Just seeing you makes their day. They wake up every day and you are the first person they wish to see. They watch everything you do. You inspire them in ways you can't imagine. There is a purpose behind all of your pain and you are going to be able to change so many lives on your journey. That is what life is all about; changing lives and having a positive impact on other people. I never knew why I went through so much in my life while I was going through it. I left my family at a young age because there is a price you have to pay on the road to success. Most people aren't willing to pay the full price. Are you? I know what it feels like not to see my mom for ten years on Mother's Days. I know what it feels like to miss ten years of Father's Days with my dad. Ten years of missing birthdays and so many other important occasions. That hurts. I know what it feels like to see your teammates with their parents at every game while you don't have a parent in the stands. You have to pay the full price for success, but there is a reward for it. I had no idea that when I left home at thirteen years old that I would be considered one of the greatest leaders ever in the history of Michigan State Athletics. But what if I would have given up? I'm encouraging you not to give up. There are so many great things that are going to come out of your struggles. When God told me, "I set this up just for you" I believe that He meant, "You have no idea the impact I am going to allow you to have on the lives of so many people." Up to this point in my life, I thought I was doing so many things through basketball. I have learned that I was never doing anything through basketball. I was doing things with a basketball. Everything I ever did was through Christ who strengthens me. So don't give up. Understand that it's not about you. Keep going no matter what and know that in order for you to be successful in life, you have to be Purpose Driven.

Purpose Principles

1. Focusing on what you did in the past can cause you to lose sight of the present.

2. When you believe what other people say about you, you will become whatever they call you.

3. The pressure of what others expect of you never bothers you when you have higher expectations for yourself.

4. Everything you go through in life has nothing to do with you; it has everything to do with the people you were born to reach.

5. When you don't give up and keep going, you accomplish things you never even dreamed of.

EPILOGUE

Life is not about how much money you have, how famous you are, what kind of car you drive or how big the house may be that you live in. Life is about figuring out why you were born and fulfilling that purpose for the rest of your life to the best of your ability. Each and every one of us has something special that we were born to do. However, the problem is in overcoming all the obstacles it takes to get there.

I wrote this book to encourage all of you to keep going regardless of the circumstances. As you read my book, you saw that I went through a great deal in my life and sometimes I couldn't figure out why. It wasn't until I began to realize that life is not about what you go through; life is about why you go through. When you figure out why you went through what you went through, what you went through will make more sense to you. Understanding why you went through doesn't make those situations any easier to deal with but it will make you embrace your struggles instead of being afraid of them.

I want to encourage you all to understand that you will make it through everything you think was designed to break you. Most of the things I thought were designed to break me down were actually there to build me up. Giving up is always an option in everything you face in life. However, that is an option I'm going to inspire you to NEVER choose. Giving up will not allow you to reach your full potential and discover what is truly inside of you. You will make it through. It might not seem that way right now, but if you keep fighting, you will accomplish more than you could ever imagine.

We are all going to go through trials on the way to fulfilling our purpose. The trials we encounter are not meant to break us, they are meant to make us. In essence, we experience our trials to make us into who we need to be so we can accomplish whatever it is that we are born to do. We are often afraid to tell other people about our obstacles because we don't want them to judge us. Most of the time not sharing our obstacles is our pride that gets in the way. When we don't talk about trials, it is because we don't understand that there could be millions who need to hear our stories so that they can see that they're not the only ones going through challenges.

It doesn't matter where we were born. What matters is who and what we were born to be. You may have been born in poverty, you may be homeless, your parents may have given up on you or the ones who said they loved you may have turned their backs on you. Nothing may seem to be going your way. Through any situation you're going through, know that you can and will succeed if you don't give up. Eric Thomas has a saying, "No story, No glory." The glory isn't in who you are now, the glory is in everything you're currently facing and will face to get to where and who you need to be. There is greater for your life than what you are experiencing right now. I hope that after having read this book you are motivated, inspired and encouraged to never give up in times of adversity. Be encouraged to continue to go through what you're going through because on the other side of all your pain, there is a prize—a prize that will inspire those around you and even people you may never come in contact with. The impact will be that big. Continue to fight, never give up and although giving up may be an option. I am a living example of what happens when you never give up. My purpose in life is to help make sure that giving up is an option you NEVER choose.

Journal

Journal

Journal

Journal

Journal

Journal

_____

_____

_____

_____

_____

_____

_____

_____

_____

_____

_____

_____

_____

_____

_____

Journal

_____

_____

_____

_____

_____

_____

_____

_____

_____

_____

_____

_____

_____

_____

_____

_____

Journal

_____

_____

_____

_____

_____

_____

_____

_____

_____

_____

_____

_____

_____

_____

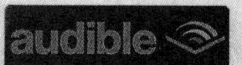

ERIC THOMAS AND ASSOCIATES, LLC.

EDUCATION CONSULTING | ATHLETIC DEVELOPMENT | EXECUTIVE COACHING | PROFESSIONAL DEVELOPMENT

"WHEN YOU WANT TO SUCCEED AS BAD AS YOU WANT TO BREATHE..." EDUCATORS, CORPORATIONS, AND ORGANIZATIONS AROUND THE WORLD SEEK OUT ETA IN RELIANCE ON THE REPUTATION OF TRUST, QUALITY, INTEGRITY, AND DEDICATION THAT HAS BEEN ESTABLISHED BY THE BRAND. HERE AT ETA, WE UNDERSTAND THE NECESSITY OF EQUIPPING OUR CLIENTS WITH THE TOOLS THEY NEED TO NOT ONLY RESPOND TO CHANGES AND ADVERSITIES IN THEIR ENVIRONMENT, BUT ALSO ADAPT IN A WAY THAT WILL ENABLE THEM TO STAY AHEAD OF THE COMPETITION, THRIVE IN THE MIDST OF MISFORTUNE, AND AROUSE THEM TO INITIATE THEIR OWN MOVEMENT OF MOTIVATION AND ENCOURAGEMENT IN THEIR OWN COMMUNITIES, ORGANIZATIONS, AND SUBGROUPS.

THE ETA METHOD IS COMPRISED OF THREE ESSENTIAL THREADS:

STEP 1 - SEED → STEP 2 - GROW → STEP 3 - INSPIRE

ONE-ON-ONE COACHING WITH ET EMAIL COACHING@ETINSPIRES.COM